Florence Shopping Guide

by Carol Senatore

Foreword

Who is better suited to writing a guide for shopping in Florence than a local resident who has lived here for over 20 years? That's me — a New Yorker who moved to Florence in 1990 - and I hope to help make your shopping experience easier and more satisfying.

Lots of tourists fall into the trap of just going down the main drag, ending up in shops that only cater to foreigners. Any yet, there's so much great stuff right around the corner. This guide will help you find it.

The idea for a Florence shopping guide came about as a result of my website **florencewebguide.com** (*please visit my site — there are some great pages — but do bear in mind that it is still very much a work-in-progress*).

In my wanderings downtown, I couldn't help but notice all the visitors rushing around with shopping bags. I came to a realization: **vacationers love to shop in Florence**!

So what a shame to think that they are missing out on local artisan workshops, convenient stores for designer clothes, and the quaint boutiques that locals know and love.

I decided to create a guide to fill people in about this type of authentic Florence shopping.

Oh, and BTW, this selection of shops is based exclusively on my honest opinion. Lots of guides are full of information merely because the businesses have paid to be included in the book. That is NOT the case with the Florence Shopping Guide. This is the real deal: only worthy shops are included.

So what makes for a 'worthy' shop?

First of all, the main focus of this guide is on **locally manufactured goods** which represent Italian style and quality. You'll find out where you can buy goods that are hand-manufactured by Florentine artisans, such as leather bags, shoes, gloves, belts, traditional Florentine paper, 18k gold jewelry, ceramics, and more.

Secondly, a worthy shop is one which offers **reasonable prices, pleasant and professional service and which has an authentic Florentine atmosphere.** These are aspects that I think most people appreciate.

Lastly, I've included shops that offer **something special**, but which most tourists probably wouldn't find on their own (I know, that's what a guide is *supposed* to do, but not all of them actually do it!).

There's more though.

Visitors to Florence love buying **Italian designer name goods.** So, no guide would be complete without lots of information about where to get bargains on Florentine (Gucci, Pucci, Ferragamo, Cavalli, etc) and Italian (Armani, Prada, Max Mara, etc.) label clothes and bags. There are tons of pages dedicated to this.

There's also a chapter called **'Special Mention'** (I think you'll really love this part!). 'Special Mention' tells about Florence's most unique and original shops – the 'not-to-be-missed' ones. These shops are all one-of-a-kind and have a detailed description explaining why.

And there's a heck of a lot more...

You'll get all the information you need about all types of **markets, department stores, chain stores, historical shops,** and even **fringe shopping** (shopping areas that are popular with Florentine residents but 'off the beaten path' for tourists).

Let me briefly tell you how I gathered all this information.

First, I used **my own experience**. After all, I live here and go shopping in Florence all the time so I don't get caught in any tourist traps.

Secondly, I got new ideas by pestering all my **friends** and **acquaintances** to find out where they shop for good deals. Their input was invaluable.

And lastly (and this was the hardest part) **I went down each and every street** in downtown Florence and also the outer neighborhoods, went into each shop, and checked out the goods and compared prices.

This took me several months, but I think the finished product is worth it. I'm able to provide a selection of the shops that I think people will appreciate the most and which offer the most competitive prices.

Florence is a city that has always thrived on its craftsmen and women, artisans working with leather, ceramics, gold, decorated paper, embroidery, and of course, clothes and fashion in all spheres.

With this in mind, my philosophy is that shopping in Florence isn't just about buying things to take home with you, but is also about getting to know the city and its heritage.

Visiting workshops, seeing how goods are made, recognizing the quality of handcrafted products, all help to enrich a visitor's sojourn (whether you buy anything or not).

Therefore, my hope is that this guide will enhance your visit to Florence and help you to really know this great town and all it has to offer.

If you have any comments or suggestions about this guide, you can contact me at *www.florencewebguide.com* – it would be great to hear from you.

Happy shopping!

Carol

An informative note: *this book has been prepared without any maps or photos to ensure the maximum compactness. A folding map will be much more helpful to navigate the downtown streets and find addresses (**free ones are available at tourist information offices – see 'maps' below**). I felt that it was more useful to dedicate space to provide as much helpful information as possible, rather than adding photos of shop fronts or clothing racks. Please use the Internet addresses provided to have a visual idea of the shop and what it sells.*

Handy things to know

Best time to visit Florence

To avoid the busy season but still be in Florence with mild weather, September- October and April-June are the best times. **If shopping is your main interest though, you're better off coming at the start of the official sales period.** All stores and outlet shops offer up to 50% off starting from the second week of January through to the end of February and from the second week of July through to the end of August. For the best finds try to be in Florence at the very beginning of the sales period – by the end of the month (or even the first week) all the good stuff will probably be gone!

Shop opening hours

Most shops are open **9:30 – 1:00** and then **3:30 – 7:30,** and are closed on Monday mornings and Sundays all day. In July and August things change: shops open on Monday mornings and close instead on Saturday afternoons. In August in particular many shops are closed for vacation or have a reduced timetable.

However, more and more shops (especially in the downtown area) are getting away from the traditional timetable. Many no longer close at lunchtime and some stay open on Sundays too. I try to give as much information as possible about each shop's opening hours. However, if you want to be sure to find a store open, **shopping during the 'standard' times is your best bet**.

Also, shops – especially those run by only one or two people – often take liberties with their schedules. A shop owner may close for 45 minutes to have a quick lunch for example. If a shop closes for just a short time, it's customary to put a sign on the door saying **'torno subito'** ('be back soon'), in which case the shop will normally re-open within half an hour. If you are going out of your way to visit a particular shop (ie a store that is **'off the beaten track'**), it may be a good idea to phone first.

Shop etiquette

It's common courtesy in Florence for shop-assistants to welcome you to the shop when you walk in ('Buongiorno' or 'Buona sera'). To exchange the courtesy, simply repeat ('Buongiorno' or 'Buona sera').

The same goes for when you leave – it's considered a bit rude to just walk out. A pleasant 'Grazie' is appropriate (even, or better yet, *especially* if you haven't bought anything!).

Shop assistants will also try to help you in your purchase (especially in small boutiques). They consider this part of their job, and often they'll come right over to you and ask what you are looking for. This might come across as pushy to some shoppers, but really it is just the way things are done here.

Shop assistants can be very helpful and are particularly knowledgeable about fashion, clothing, sizes, etc. so it could be a good idea to make the most of their assistance. If, on the other hand, you're the kind of person who just wants to browse on your own, you can just say so nicely and you'll be left to do so.

Phone numbers

Numbers are given for local dialling, starting with the Florence area code (055). Your mobile phone service however may require that you make the call as if it were an international number being phoned from your country. To do so, you need to first dial **'+' (international code)** and then **'39' (the Italy country code)**, and then the number given in the guide.

Addresses

There are two types of street numbers in Florentine addresses: 'regular' numbers and **'red'** numbers. 'Red' numbers are used for commercial activities and are usually written in red on the store front. In written addresses 'red' numbers are specified with an 'r' (eg via del Corso, **7r**). 'Regular' numbers can either be a residential home or a business, and don't usually have a letter after the number.

So, when looking for an address, don't get confused when you see two different sets of numbers while walking up a street, if the address you want is a 'red' number, only pay attention to those. If it's a 'regular' number, just ignore the 'red' numbers and follow the others ('regular' numbers are usually written in black or blue).

The Station

All references to the 'train station' refer to the Santa Maria Novella station right in the heart of town. There are two main entrances, one in via Alamanni and one in Largo Alinari. The via

Alamanni side of the station is referred to as the **'tram side'** since this is where the tram stops, and the Largo Alinari side is referred to as the **'pharmacy side'** since just inside this entrance there is a 24 hour pharmacy.

Maps

A free **map of Florence** with a useful street index is available at tourist information offices. Tourist offices are in **piazza Stazione 4** (just outside the station, near the traffic roundabout on the right of the stony back of Santa Maria Novella church), **via Cavour 1r** and **piazza San Giovanni** (near the Duomo).

You can also pick up a very useful **bus map** at the ATAF (the bus company of Florence) customer service office; this map covers a vaster area than the free city map. There are two **ATAF offices** in the station: the main one is at the front of the station in **Piazza Stazione**, at the top of the bus-taxi ramp under the station clock (Mon – Sat 7.30 – 7.30, Sun closed). The second is in **via Alamanni 20r**: go down the steps leaving the station, turn right, go past a Conad supermarket, a florist and a post office. The ATAF office is next (Mon – Sat 7.15 – 7, Sun closed).

Buses

The Florence Shopping Guide provides very detailed information about finding bus-stops and using buses to get around. As this guide goes to print though, the ATAF bus company has been just privatized. This could bring about changes to some of the lines in the very near future. For the latest information refer to the ATAF website **www.ataf.net**, the ATAF offices cited above, or the tourist offices.

Getting around downtown

Without a doubt **walking is the best option**. Florence is small and very pretty so strolling from one area to the next is a pleasure. BUT, wear comfortable shoes — the cobblestone streets are no fun in heels!

Alternatively, **you can take a bus**. The mini-buses (lines C1, C2, C3 and D) are particularly useful since they are the only public transport that goes into the heart of town, up and down the narrow roads. Mini buses are truly 'mini' though and can get very crowded. Buy bus tickets (€1,20 for 90 minutes) before boarding at newsstands, tobacco stores and coffee shops/bars. When you get on the bus you have to stamp the ticket which becomes valid for 90 minutes from the time it was stamped. Daily tickets are available too. See *www.ataf.net* for more information.

Taxis abound and are a viable alternative if you want to get somewhere fast and comfortably. Flagging down a taxi is not allowed in Florence, you need to get one at a taxi stand. There are stands at the Santa Maria Novella train station and in several other main squares. You can also call for a taxi at 055 4390 or 055 4499 (note: the cab will arrive with a few euros charge already on the meter for the call service).

Table of Contents

Special Mention Shops

This section provides a short list of shops which, in my opinion, set themselves apart. Why?

Firstly, these stores are all **unique** and have **a strong individual identity** – basically, there's no other shop like them in town.

And secondly, these shops have a particular **connection to Florence** in one way or another, which makes them deserving of a special nod in this Florence shopping guide.

Photos of Florence

1) Torrini
where via Condotta, 20r (near piazza Signoria)
store hours 9 – 7
phone   055 48 01 57

Of all the shops I've seen, this is my favorite.
Torrini is the exclusive owner of some of the most spectacular photographs of Florence and its history. You can't find these images anywhere else. Apart from having some of the most original shots of the symbols of Florence (the David, the Duomo, piazza Signoria, the Ponte Vecchio), you can also find romantic and poetic pictures of what Florence and Italy used to be like. Photos date from 1944 til today.

Price range: small photos start at 13€

Tip: the most popular shots have been put onto postcards which you can buy for €1.50 each – a great and inexpensive way to take home these one-of-a-kind memories of Florence or to send to family and friends. You can only find these postcards in this store as the photographers do not permit any other vendors to sell their images.

www.torrinifotogiornalismo.it

Renaissance Leather Workshop

2) Florence Leather School *(Scuola del Cuoio)*

where via San Giuseppe 5r (behind the Santa Croce church just off the piazza)
store hours every day 9:30 – 6 pm (closed on Sundays from November to March)
phone   055 24 45 34

The Florence Leather School is the ultimate visitors' experience for anybody who is interested in artisan craftsmanship of the first degree.

The school both teaches how to become a master leatherworker as well as sells its spectacular leather goods made on the premises. The artisans and apprentices alongside them carry about their business of creating leather bags, wallets and other items out in the open for all the customers to see (the shop and work area overlap in some areas).

Bags are the school's 'forte' – and these are magnificent – but you can also buy jackets, wallets, belts and briefcases as well as small leather items like bookmarks, coin cases, key chains, etc.

I call the school a Renaissance workshop for two reasons: it is located in the monastery of the Santa Croce church, an antique and historical Renaissance setting, and because the craftspeople at the school produce the leather goods using the age-old tools of leather workers of the past, manual equipment rather than modern electronic machinery.

This is Italian creativity and craftsmanship of the highest level – true artistry.

www.scuoladelcuoio.com

Personalized Jewelry

3) Alisi
where via Porta Rossa, 60r (near piazza Santa Trinità)
store hours Tue – Sat 10 – 1:30 and 3 - 7
phone 055 21 82 31

Alisi is a unique and very special jewelry shop. Susanna and Camilla Alisi, Florentines, are jewelers who custom-make and personalize jewelry pieces in gold, silver, and other materials. The boutique also has items in the shop inspired by Florence and its history. Some examples: a diamond Brunelleschi dome pendant, a charm in the shape of Santo Spirito church, or replicas of Florentine Medieval and Renaissance style rings.

They have also created a collection dedicated to the antique guilds of Florence which reproduces the crests and symbols of these institutions in modern jewelry – the cufflinks in this collection are exquisite and make a great gift – ask to be shown these beautiful pieces.

Alisi also has a special line, 'the little prince' dedicated to the world of fables, children and animals – these make wonderful personalized gifts for children (and adults!) because they can design a piece to represent the personality of the person it's meant for.

It's hard to do justice to Alisi's beautiful products with words, so check out their site or just pop in to admire in person.

www.alisigioielli.com

Cutting-Edge of Fashion

4) Luisa
where via Roma, 19 (near piazza Repubblica)
store hours 10 – 7:30 closed Sundays
phone 055 90 64 116

Luisa is considered a sort-of shrine to fashion. The store is known locally, nationally, and world-wide within fashion circles.

The shop might also be considered a contemporary museum thanks to its shop window which is probably more famous than the shop itself. The shop window changes at each season and is considered one of the most innovative and avant-garde window displays in Italy.

All the clothes, shoes, and accessories sold here are cool, modern and at the fore-front of fashion. If Lady Gaga came shopping to Florence, this is where she'd go.

You can certainly find famous Italian brands at Luisa's but a lot of the designers are also foreign since often it's the British or Japanese designer who comes up with the type of eccentric styles that Luisa is famous for (Italians are great at fashion but tend to be more traditional).

Prices: from very high to even higher

www.luisaviaroma.com

A One-of-a-Kind Cobbler

5) Mondo Albion
where via Nazionale, 121 A/R
store hours see below
phone 055 28 24 51

This must be the only shop of its kind in the world. The owner, Albion, is a free-spirit who is an artist, poet (he sells a small pamphlet on the secrets to life in the shop) and – here's the part that might interest you – a shoe maker. Indeed, he is regarded as a master shoe craftsman.

When you walk into the store you are immediately immersed in shoes (mostly all black) – on shelves, on the work table, on the floors, hanging up – there is absolutely no organization to it all (that I can see). Some examples: shoes with an octagonal heel, platform shoes with a hand-painted picture on the side, black leather shoes with colored leather patchwork added, and so on. Like the man himself, the shoes and boots in the shop are artistic, highly eccentric and inimitable.

The work areas in the shop are behind high shelves so you may walk in and not see any shop assistant. Then, you hear a voice shout out and Albion pops up (the grey hair, beard and mustache, baggy clothes and slippers will let you know it's him). According to Albion, the best time to go is in the afternoons after 4 pm to be sure the shop will be open.

Getting back to shoes, if you can find a pair that you like and that fit, you will be very happy with this truly unique and one-of-a-kind Florentine shoe.

Prices: usually not written, you ask the price and then you can bargain a bit. By-and-large I'd say from €100 up, hand-painted shoes in €200 range.

www.mondoalbion.it

Paper-mache Craftsmanship

6) Alice Masks
where via Faenza, 72r (right off via Nazionale)
store hours 9 – 1 and 3:30 – 7:30 (Sundays closed)
phone 055 28 73 70

Alice Masks has been creating splendid paper-mache pieces in Florence since 1973 and is the only shop of its kind in the city. Agostino Dessi is the original mask-maker who now works together with his daughter Alice. Besides selling their pieces to the general public, father and daughter also produce masks and props for theater, festivals, carnivals, and films.

This small shop has a real workshop feel. The entrance is full of a variety of finished pieces whereas the back area is dedicated to production where you can see the works being made and painted.

You can find masks and paper-mache sculptures of famous Florentine images which are of exceptionally high quality (some replicas of Michelangelo's David are remarkable in their likeness to the original).

Alice Masks also offers courses with hands-on paper-mache workshops – see website for details.

www.alicemasks.com

Shop-cum-Archeologic Site-cum-Coffee Bar

8) A Piedi Nudi nel Parco (aka: PN\P) ('barefoot in the park')
Where via del Proconsolo, 1n (near piazza San Firenze)
Store hours 10:30 – 7:30, Sundays 12 – 7:30 (in summer closed on Sundays)
Phone 055 21 80 99

A must-see for one main reason: the first room just as you walk into the store has a glass floor under which you can see the ruins of a Roman settlement.   How many stores can brag about something like that?

Another unique factor is the bar in the store – in the same room as the Roman ruins - so you can have a cocktail or a coffee before you browse.

The key word to describe this store is 'dark'. The lighting is low, the décor is dark and almost all the clothes are black (very New York/Berlin inspired).   PN\P is known for its avant-garde materials and is always searching for the most contemporary fabrics which are then sewn into some of the most inventive garments you're likely to see in town.

This shop has only women's clothes.   The store dedicated to men's clothes is in via Santa Margherita, 2r (in front of Dante's house).

Note: *since this is a shop and not a museum, a drink at the bar is mandatory if you go into the store just to see the archeological ruins.*

www.pnp-firenze.com

Second-Hand Designer Bags and Clothes

7) Usato & Balla (since **1988**)
Where via E. Mayer, 6 -10r (near piazza Leopoldo) **(off the beaten track)**
store hours 9 – 12:30 and 3:30 – 7
(closed Sundays and sometimes Monday mornings, call to check)
phone 055 48 05 85

An ingenious shop that sells only second-hand designer bags, shoes, and clothes, from the last 2-3 fashion seasons (these are not vintage items). This is the trick: many items in the store are practically new because they come from the world of entertainment (eg. wives of soccer players from the Florence team, Italian celebrities, pop singers, etc). You can make some great finds here on Florentine designers, such as Gucci shoes for under €100 or a Pucci dress for €120.

There's an especially large section for elegant evening gowns – a great occasion to purchase something very special at affordable prices. Why spend a ton for a dress you might only wear a few times (or once!)? Here you can buy a prestigious brand, look great and save your hard earned bucks.

The store also has a section for **plus-sizes**.

Designer bags too are all recent models, going back 3 years at the most (no vintage). Some examples of prices I saw: Prada bag €53, Moschino bag €44 and little purse €32, Ferré bag €70.

How to get there: short taxi ride from station (10 mins) or bus 14 direction 'Careggi' or 'Tolentino' – from the station the bus stop is on the pharmacy side, across the street near the traffic light in Largo Alinari (in front of 'Fabiani' jewelers). Take bus to 'Milanesi' stop, via Mayer is the street parallel to v. Milanesi.

www.usatoeballa.it

Marble and Bronze Statues

9) Pietro Bazzanti & Son (since **1822**)
Where Lungarno Corsini, 44 r
Store hours Mon – Sat 9 – 12:30 and 3 – 7:30
Phone 055 21 56 49

This is a historic art gallery that specializes in replicas of famous statues, many of which are found in the museums in Florence. Sculptures are made in bronze, marble and also stone.

The reproductions that you will see here are so well done it feels as if you are being allowed to walk through a museum without any ropes stopping you from getting close to the artwork.

You can see replicas of well-known works by famous Florentine artists such as Michelangelo, Donatello, Verrocchio and others. The gallery – which is very big and situated in an elegant street along the Arno - has over 5,000 sculptures.

Often the sculptures are done to scale but the store also has a large number of small classical bronzes of well-known pieces that can easily be transported.

The gallery also sells original works of art by 19th and 20th century Florentine and Italian artists. Whether you would like a sculpture, statue, or fountain for your patio, garden area or living room, or just want to admire this type of art work up close, the Bazzanti gallery is definitely worth visiting. Small bronzes start at about €150.

www.galleriabazzanti.it

Historical Shops

Certain shops have obtained the status of 'historical shops' due to their importance and longevity. You can find a complete list of these at the Florence city council website *www.esercizistorici.it*.

Here's a short list of the most notable historical shops.

Antique Pharmacy and Perfumes

Officina Profumo Farmaceutica di Santa Maria Novella (since **1612**)
where via della Scala, 16 (station area)
store hours 9:30 – 7:30
phone 055 21 62 76

One of the world's first pharmacies was started by Dominican Friars in the 13th century and became an authorized seller of medicinal remedies in 1612. Today the officina is more popular for its perfumes, creams and scented soaps. Many of the essences and scents are still produced according to the formulas developed in the Renaissance for Caterina de' Medici. A great place for gifts.

The premises of the pharmacy are opulent. From the outside it looks like just an antique building (there's no shop sign). Inside, the rooms are very large and elegant. There are ceiling frescoes and marble floors that date to 1840. The walls too are frescoed with biblical scenes by a Florentine artist going back to the 15th century. **Of all the historical shops, this is the one not to be missed** – if only to soak up the shop's unique atmosphere.

www.smnovella.com

Wigs and Make-up

Filistrucchi (since **1720**)
where via Verdi, 9 (Santa Croce area)
store hours 8:30 – 12:30 and 3 – 7 closed Mon morning, Sat afternoon and all day Sun)
phone 055 23 44 901

A family of wig-makers who have carried over this specialized art from generation to generation. In the 1700's the family business started out as a barber shop, and at that time it was the barber who also made wigs. This led to Filistrucchi developing and perfecting the niche that it's famous for today: wigs made of natural hair. The shop is also specialized in cosmetics and make-up artistry – a perfect place to go to get ready for Halloween, Mardi Gras or Florence's carnival period. The shop is still in its original location, having survived two floods of the Arno, and its antique store front and ambience is worth a visit.

www.filistrucchi.com

British Merchandise

Old England Stores (since **1924**)
where via Vecchietti, 28r (p. Repubblica area)
store hours 10 - 7:30   Sun closed
phone 055 21 19 83

This shop was originally opened to satisfy the expats living in Florence who wanted things from home. Today, it is more likely to be frequented by Florentines who appreciate a change from Italian tastes and styles. The shop has two sections: foodstuff and clothing. Popular items in the first section are the English biscuits and jams and American style cereal and cake mixes. Clothing wise, you can find Shetland lambs wool sweaters, flannels, Harris tweed and classic rain jackets and trench coats.

Haberdashery

Quercioli e Lucherini (since **1895**)
where via Porta Rossa, 45r (p. Repubblica area)
store hours 9 − 1 and 3 − 7   closed Mon morning and Sun
phone 055 29 20 35

Florentines like to look good and wear stylish clothing, and this doesn't stop at the surface. Even one's socks, boxer shorts, and wool undershirt have to look good. This old Florentine notions shop will show you what I mean. Here you can find Italian quality items such as intimate apparel, hosiery, pajamas, slips, undershirts, and every type of brassiere to resolve your wardrobe problems (eg strapless, with no-see straps, natural-color to be invisible with sheer clothes, and so on).

Tassels and Trimmings

Passamaneria Valmar (since **1960**)
where via Porta Rossa, 53r (p. Repubblica area)
store hours 9 − 7   Sat opens at 10 Sun closed
phone 055 28 44 93

Valmar carries on a traditional Florentine craft that is becoming rarer and rarer: the making of fancy tassels and trimmings. The colors in the shop, deep burgundy and gold, are the colors of Renaissance Florence. A third generation family business, the Lapi's produce their goods in the workshop above the store. Find also embroidered velvet pillows, bracelets for curtains, centerpieces, footstools, table runners, and similar items for the home.

Porcelain Dinnerware

Richard Ginori (since 1735)
where via dei Rondinelli, 17r
store hours Mon – Sat 10 – 1 and 2 – 7   Sun closed
phone 055 21 00 41

This historical shop originates from the Doccia porcelain manufactory founded in 1735 by Carlo Ginori in Sesto Fiorentino, just outside Florence.   The Ginori heirs continued through the generations producing elegant and sought after porcelain pieces for the dinner table and home until 1896. A partnership was then formed with Richard from Milan – a ceramics manufacturer, giving us today's pedigree shop famous the world over.

www.richardginori1735.com

Antique Items

Parenti (since 1865)
where via Tornabuoni, 93r
store hours Mon – Sat 10 – 1 & 2 – 7   Sun closed
phone 055 21 44 38

The great-grandfather of the current owner of this antiques boutique in Florence used to serve King Vittorio Emanuele and his family. In the store today you can still see the Royal crest granted to Parenti for providing the service of seeking out the rare, original and valuable objects that a regal household would require. The store is still thriving today, serving its elite clientele with antique items of every nature.

www.parentifirenze.it

Vintage Music Shop

Occasioni Musicali (since 1963)
where via dell'Oriuolo, 33r (behind piazza Duomo)
store hours Mon – Sat 10:30 – 13:30 & 4 – 8   Sun closed
phone 055 23 47 008

This shop is considered 'historic' due to its significant cultural legacy. The violinist, Ugo Guerrini opened the store in 1963 and it soon became a reference point for countless Florentine musicians, selling, buying, trading second hand instruments, sheet music and records. Today, you can also find a large assortment of music and non-music related collectibles and antique items.

Apothecary

Bizzarri (since 1842)
where via Condotta, 32r (off to the side of piazza Signoria)
store hours Mon – Sat 10:30 – 13:30 and 4 – 8   Sun closed
phone 055 21 15 80

When you open the creaky wooden door to this shop and you hear the ding of the metal bell signaling that someone has entered the store, you'll feel like you've been transported back to another century. It's remarkable how this shop has managed to preserve a 19th century atmosphere – this alone is worth the visit. The store sells dyes, herbs, rare spices, smelling salts, perfumed oils, articles for restoration of artwork and lots of other hard-to-find items for specialist needs.

Frames

Cornici Campani (since **1889**)
where via dei Servi, 22r (near Duomo)
store hours 9 – 12:30 & 3 – 7:30 Sun closed
phone 055 21 69 84

This historical woodworking shop specializes in handcrafted frames in all sizes and styles. The shop's founder, Gino Campani, was the esteemed frame-maker to Florence's most renowned painters at the turn of the century. The shop hasn't lost its reputation and still offers the same workmanship. Small frames go for about €25 and would be perfect for special vacation photos of Florence.

See also, in other sections of this guide, additional historic shops:
- **Giulio Giannini & Figlio** under 'Florentine Papergoods'
- **Mannina** under 'Artisan Leather Workshops'

Leather

Artisan Leather Workshops

Florence is known for its fine leather craftsmanship and there are still plenty of workshops producing wonderful hand-made items.

The pages that follow provide a list of shops where you can purchase leather goods which are made by the shop owners, often on the premises in the work area in the store.

Bags, wallets, and other

Gioia Chiara
where via della Scala, 11r (station area)
store hours Mon to Sat 9 – 1 & 2:30 - 7:30
phone 055 29 07 72

This type of family-run leather production is getting rarer and rarer. You can buy good quality hand-made Italian designed leather bags, wallets and belts at extremely reasonable prices.

The family (in the business for 60 years and three generations) especially like working with fun colors, making bags and wallets in lots of bright hues as well as the classic brown and black leather.

Sells bags of all sizes and types, wallets, briefcases, make-up pouches, belts, key chains and other small items. Gift ideas in leather starting at €5, wallets starting at €20, bags at €35.

www.gioiachiara.it

Dantesca leather
where via Santa Margherita, 13r (just off busy via del Corso)
store hours 10 – 7:30 (Saturday opens at 11)
phone 055 28 91 87

This shop looks more like a workshop than a store, the goods are stacked here and there on shelves and hooks while in the middle the work is carried out. Dantesca is on a tiny side-street that you might never walk into if you have no reason for going there.

Dantesca has very good prices on a large selection of handbags as well as many other leather goods. Medium sized handbags about €40 – 50.

Once you're there, you can also admire the **11th century Santa Margherita de' Cerchi** church (called 'Dante's church' since he was supposedly married there, and his muse, Beatrice, is said to be buried there).

20:12 Gallery
where via dei Federighi, 10r (near the Museo Marino Marini, street parallel to via del Moro)
store hours Mon to Sat 10 – 1 & 3 - 8
phone 055 27 76 401

Dimitri Villoresi is the owner and mind behind this leather workshop/store/art gallery.

About the leather goods: Dimitri prides himself on the fact that he does not use any machinery, all the stitching and workmanship is done by hand. He uses the most traditional ways of working leather to create contemporary looking bags and small leather items. The items are modern because you don't see the customary beige, brown or black so much but rich reds or bright greens and other colors. Also the cut, design and style of the goods are original and creative. The leather too is particularly soft and buttery.

The gallery: the shop also houses exhibitions of contemporary artists – Italian and foreign – whose art is dedicated to craftsmanship and artisans. Dimitri's project is to combine long-standing traditions of hands-on workmanship with a modern twist, an innovative perspective.

Sells: bags, belts, wallets, eye glass cases, and other small leather goods. Small items start at €60, bags €150 and up.

www.ventidodicigallery.it

Small leather items (boxes, coin purses, eye-glass cases)

Il Bussetto
where via Palazzuolo, 136r (near station)
store hours 9 – 1 & 3:30 – 7:30 (Closed Sundays)
phone 055 29 06 97

Giuseppe Fanara has been working in Florence for over 20 years. His store is a combination shop/workshop that sells the popular Florentine coin case, card holders, glass cases, and other small items. In the shop you can see Giuseppe at work amidst pieces of rawhide leather, oils and dyes.

His workmanship is sought out: Armani and Moschino – among other important labels – have commissioned him to produce leather products to be sold under their name (see scrapbook in store with other designer commissions).

The coin case, known as 'il tacco' (the heel), is by far the most popular item. There are 3 sizes and they start at €34 for the smallest. This typical Florence coin carrier – made by molding the leather with water (there are no stitches at all) - is an ingenious work. The case is small and light to fit in your pocket without being bulky (it's used more by men than women) and, although it's tiny, it holds lots of change, which – when opened – comes spilling out into its own 'cup', which folds back into itself when you close it up. A way to carry change with a real touch of class, and a fantastic gift idea too (can be hand-branded with initials for a personal touch).

www.ilbussettofirenze.com

Cellini (since **1952**)
where via Sant'Egidio, 31r (near piazza Santa Maria Nuova)
store hours 9 – 1 and 3:30 – 7:30 (Closed Sundays)
phone 055 24 53 35

Cellini's produce (in the rear of the shop) a wide variety of small items made in different types and qualities of leather. The trademark Cellini product is the leather cigar case, but they also have a large selection of boxes of all types and sizes, eye glass cases, and other office and desk items. From time-to-time the shop also sells vintage designer bags.

Like so many Florentine artisans, Cellini too is a supplier of hand-made Italian leather items sold abroad to luxury retail stores which then charge quite a bit more for these goods than what you pay here in town. Average prices €20 - 40.

www.pelletteriefiorentine.it

Footwear

Note: *see also 'Special Mention' section for the shoemaker shop*
'Mondo Albion'

Mannina (since 1942)
where via Guicciardini, 16r (between Pitti Palace and Ponte Vecchio)
store hours 10 - 7
phone 055 28 28 95

The Mannina family have been making shoes since 1942 (see a small historical display cabinet in store showing shoes that Mrs. Mannina made for her granddaughter).

The store walls are covered in newspaper clippings and photos which testify to the expertise of these historical Florentine shoemakers.

Mannina's classic lines are shoes in traditional brown and black leather for men. Large selection for women too, with more variety and colors — still in classic styles that don't go out of fashion.

See shoes being handmade in the Mannina workshop around the corner from store: leave store and go in direction towards Ponte Vecchio, make first left. Workshop is on the left, via Barbadori, 19r.

Prices: from €150 up for ladies shoes, men's handcrafted shoes from €250

www.manninafirenze.com

Calzature Francesco da Firenze

where via Santo Spirito, 62r (Just over the Ponte alla Carraia bridge on south side)
store hours 10 – 1 & 4 – 7:30 (Sundays closed)
phone 055 21 24 28

A small family run business, they make the shoes and sell them in this very simple shop. The store carries several different types of shoes but only a few pairs of each. They are not over-stocked but tend to have few items of the more classic popular styles.

Prices are reasonable and they often have some sale items at good bargains too. This is the kind of shop where you might not find anything at all that suits you, but, if lucky, you could also make a great find.

Calzaturificio "Laudato" (since 1970's)

where via Santa Monica, 17r (near piazza del Carmine)
store hours Tue – Fri 10 – 1 & 4 – 7:30, Mon 4 – 7:30, Sat 10 – 1 (in summer months open all day Saturday)
phone 055 29 22 29

A wonderful workshop/store that sells one thing only: **Sandals.**

The Laudato family have perfected the art of producing simple flat walking sandals in natural leather colors (very few models come in colors other than brown, white or black). Several styles on offer for men and women, all of the casual Roman/Greek sandal type.

Laudato sandals are exported to be sold in high-end department stores abroad where they go for 3 or 4 times the price available here in Florence at the shop (between €40 – 60).

Saskia – shoes made to fit
where via di Santa Lucia, 24r (near station)
store hours 9 – 1 & 3 – 7 (closed Saturday afternoons and Sundays)
phone 055 29 32 91

A workshop where you can have shoes custom made, in the fullest sense of the term. Saskia first makes a mold of your feet, and then makes the shoes to fit comfortably around the particularities of each individual foot.   Due to the studied time-consuming work involved in making each pair of Saskia's shoes, the shoes are meant to be an investment for a lifetime (Saskia re-soles when needed). If you want to pamper yourself with luxury craftsmanship, this is the place (a pair of shoes takes a few months to make and goes for over €1000).

90% of Saskia's clients are male, as a man's shoe tends to follow a traditional style and doesn't go out of fashion. However, the workshop also satisfies requests for women's pumps and leather loafers and other ladies shoes. *All shoes made-to-order, there are no 'pre-made' shoes for sale in the shop at all – this is not a shoe store in the traditional sense but solely a workshop.*

www.saskiascarpesumisura.com

Leather Bags

It's ridiculous how many shops for leather bags there are in Florence. One thing (which most tourists don't know) that simplifies choosing the best store to buy from is this: **the majority of the shops all sell the same stuff and are not run by Florentine leather specialists.**

Here's a typical scene you will experience in one of these anonymous stores: you step foot into the store and the shop assistant (who won't be Italian but you might not be able to tell) will immediately say '50% off all prices!' '50% discount!'. Basically the prices are all marked up to make it seem that they are offering you a huge bargain.

I prefer a more straight-forward way of shopping. The shops I list don't use this system and are all run by Florentines with a history in leather goods. These are also all shops that have been around for many years — this type of longevity is a guarantee of credibility and quality work.

Stores are divided by price range. The higher the price, the more sophisticated the bag: more detailed finishings, higher-level accessories (solid brass snaps, silk lining, etc.), exclusive designs, and, softer or sturdier leather.

Under €100

1)   Simone & Pitti Idea
where via Guicciardini, 37r (near Palazzo Pitti)
store hours everyday 10:30 - 7:30
phone 055 21 05 12

This family has been in business for 50 years. The shop has an extremely large selection of classic and trendier styles for men and women. Selections range from soft calfskin bags to rugged brown robust leather briefcases and shoulder strap bags. Simone also produces their own line of elegant bags for women in shiny or printed leather.

Note: also go to the upstairs part of the store for sale items (some great bargains here!)

2) Gioia Chiara (see 'Artisan leather workshops' section for more information)
where via della Scala, 11r (nearish the station)
store hours Mon – Sat 9 – 1 & 2:30 - 7:30
phone 055 29 07 72

3) Valeria
where via Borgo Ognissanti, 148r
store hours Monday 4:30 – 8, Tue – Sat 10 – 1:30 & 4:30 - 8
phone 055 26 85 85

A retail store with (almost) wholesale prices. Large selection of leather handbags, from sporty to dressy styles. Owner used to work in leather production but now just does retail (he doesn't mind giving small discounts if you ask!). Selection mostly for women.

Between €100 – 200

1) Ottino (since 1830)
where via Porta Rossa, 69r (nearish Piazza della Repubblica)
store hours Mon 3:30 – 7:30, Tue – Sat 10 – 7:30
phone 055 21 21 39

Ottino has been producing their own quality leather bags since 1830 and used to be supplier to the Italian royal family. Styles are more traditional with most bags in brown or beige leather in conservative never-go-out-of-fashion styles. **If you want the consummate Italian bag, this is the best place.**

Bags, purses, wallets, and briefcases. Also bags in linen or canvas fabrics.

www.ottino.com

2) Umberto (since 1969)
where via Guicciardini, 114r (between Pitti Palace and Ponte Vecchio)
store hours 9 – 7 (closed Sundays)
phone 055 29 30 91

Umberto is one of the longest-standing shops for leather bags and wallets in Florence. Enormous range of styles from sporty or classic to the supremely luxurious. Designer names as well as small-scale manufacturers. Special assortment of ladies evening bags that is very impressive (gorgeous clutches decorated with Swarovski crystals).

Thanks to huge selection, good for one-stop bag shopping. Items for men and women.

3) Fontanelli (since 1860)
where via Borgo Ognissanti, 80r
store hours 9:30 – 1:30 and 3:30 – 7:30 (Closed Mon mornings and Sundays)
phone 055 28 36 79

Quality leather handbags with first-class finishings. Very varied selection with the majority of bags tending towards elegant/dressy. Fontanelli has a long-standing reputation in Florence and the company also produces for many other established Florentine labels – a sure guarantee of excellent workmanship.

A special article is the reversible leather bag, so ask in the shop to see first-hand. Workshop is nearby so can make-to-order too.

Sells large and small handbags, clutches, pouchettes, elegant knapsacks, and lovely small items such as change purses, key chains, golf ball carriers, and make-up pouches all in fine leather or other materials such as snake skin, crocodile or horse hair. Most items for women.

www.fontanellirecos.it

From €200 and up

1) Bojola
Where via dei Rondinelli, 25r (between station and Duomo)
store hours everyday 10 – 7:30 pm (closed Monday mornings)
phone 055 21 11 55

Bojola is a local brand founded in Florence in 1906, so if they're still in business after 100 years, they must be doing something right. No matter what Bojola produce, the quality is superlative and very easy to spot.

The brand is famous for its use of 'washable leather', a special quality of leather that is very soft to the touch and handsome to look at, extremely sturdy, and which can be washed in the washing machine at mild temperatures.

Women's handbags and men's briefcases are the most popular items. The shop has an impressive selection of modern large-sized ladies' shoulder bags that are elegant and refined yet still manage to be casual enough for every day use. Definitely worth a visit. Large selection for men and women.

www.bojola.it

2) Madani (since **1968**)
where   Lungarno Acciaiuoli, 28r
store hours   9:30 – 7 (Sundays closed)
phone   055 29 46 50

High -quality bags that are modern and practical for everyday use, but very eye-catching due to the bright colors (fuchsia, turquoise, orange) and contemporary designs. More small and medium-sized bags than over-sized shoulder bags. Only women's bags.

Also original gift ideas hand-made in the shop by the owner (personalized bracelets and necklaces of leather and Swarovski crystals).

www.madanifirenze.it

3) Second Skin
where via dei Neri, 83r (behind Palazzo Vecchio)
store hours Mon 1 – 7   Tue – Sat 11 – 7
phone 055 26 70 465

This is a new shop in Florence that is offering something unique. What's special about the goods is the highly personal style: a cross between vintage and avant-garde. The bags and wallets have a worn-out, beaten-up look so the leather is faded and wrinkled in parts (am I making this sound impressive? I fear not, but it is, believe me!). They also have gorgeous belts, with laser-etched designs, brass studs and other special touches that are truly original.

fb: second skin store

Leather Jackets

Ok, so you would like to take home a marvelous leather jacket. Where to begin?

Just like shops for bags, Florence is inundated with shops for leather jackets. There may even be more jacket shops than bag stores if possible!

Similarly to the bag shops though, the vast majority of these are not run by Italians or Florentines or people who have a history in the craft of leather work. However, these shops sell jackets that are – for the most part - made in Italy (it should be written on the inside label), of acceptable quality, and in popular styles. I'll call these shops 'standard leather shops'.

Alternatively, if you want to purchase from locals who have roots in the leather industry and who produce their own jackets, there are some good places to go. I'll call these shops 'a-cut-above leather shops'.

Purchasing from a 'cut-above' shop run by locals with a history in leather who take pride in their work and who want to satisfy their customers may be more satisfying than buying from a 'standard' shop. 'Cut-above' jackets are certainly a step up quality wise, and may not cost all that much more than a 'standard' jacket (and, in fact, a couple of these shops have 'final pieces' racks with the same prices as the 'standard jacket' stores (ie approx. €180 – see below).

A higher quality jacket will be made of softer and lighter leather and will have a more uniform color, more polished finishings, neater seams, and will likely be more comfortable to wear. These jackets will usually have start prices of about €250 – 300.

'A-cut-above' shops

1) La Pelle (since 1983)
where   via Guicciardini, 11r (near Ponte Vecchio)
store hours   10 – 7, Sundays & holidays 10:30 – 6:30
phone   055 29 20 31

Although this shop is on a touristy street, it's not just for tourists. In business since 1983, La Pelle has built up an excellent reputation in Florence. The shop owners Aldo and Sonia sell leather jackets of their own production so their styles are exclusive to the store. They have a wide range from classic cuts to trendier looks at competitive prices. For women there is a 'final pieces' rack near the store entrance with some great bargains.

www.lapellesrl.it

2) Atelier Classe
where   via Torta, 16r (near Santa Croce)
store hours   10 – 7, Sun. 2 – 7 (Mondays not always open)
phone   055 26 81 45

This is a workshop/shop. The owner, Mirko Michele, designs, cuts, sews and finishes the jackets (and also other articles of clothing) on the premises. The area with goods on display is miniscule, but as you walk in, just on the left, is a 'final pieces' rack with €180 jackets that are much higher quality than the standards you find all over town (the catch is that these are one-off pieces so either they have your size or they don't....).

www.atelierclasse.com

3) Noi ('us')

where via Porta Rossa, 65r (nearish p. Santa Trinità)
store hours 10 – 7 (closed Sundays)
phone 055 21 03 19

In business for over 30 years, NOI is a team of Florentine gentlemen whose passion is leather. Nino, Francesco and the others want nothing more than to find you the perfect jacket.

They have a very large selection of pieces, each one more lovely than the next: chic reversible jackets, nappa leather jackets that are soft as butter, light and soft as a feather shearling coats, the list goes on.

Just to let you know, these guys are salesmen so be prepared to be wooed. Although not too pushy, they may seem a bit brash. I'm not saying you're going to get an aggressive sales pitch, just that these guys are 100% sure that you will be satisfied with one of their jackets and they want you to feel the same (there's a guest book where you can see how many people - some well-known – are thrilled with their NOI purchase).

There is definitely room for bargaining on prices here so put your haggling shoes on.

www.noi-firenze.com

'Standard' shops

A typical 'standard' shop scenario goes like this.

You go into a shop and the jackets are priced at around €350, but the shop-assistant tells you that it's 50% off so you can get the jacket for €175.... You may even be able to haggle a bit and get the jacket for €165. This is a typical game, marking up the prices on products that are popular with tourists (bags, gold).

Generally speaking though, you can expect to spend in the €165 -175 range for a standard jacket. Of course, the leather might not be as soft, the color may have slight blemishes here and there and it might not be as light or as supple to wear as a higher-end jacket.

But if you want to spend in this price range, and you're not a stickler for these particular details, then you will have no problem finding a nice jacket in Florence.

Where to shop:

You'll probably have to look around a bit to find the jacket that feels and looks the best on you, and then negotiate for the lowest price.

There are two main areas: **the San Lorenzo market and piazza Santa Croce.**

At the market you should look around the many stalls that sell leather jackets, but also the shops in the surrounding streets. Many stall owners also have shops nearby, so the jackets at the stalls are quite similar (quality-wise) to jackets in shops around the market.

A popular 'standard' shop near the market with a large selection and fair prices is: *Michelangelo Leather*, via G.B. Zannoni 9r, tel. 055 28 54 97.

Alternatively, go to piazza Santa Croce and the nearby streets. The selection is very similar to San Lorenzo so if you're short on time, just choose one area to look around (San Lorenzo has the greater number of stalls/shops and is just slightly cheaper).

A tip: via S. Giuseppe, leading away from Santa Croce (looking at the statue of Dante, it's the street parallel to the church on your left), has the shops with the lowest bargain rack prices since this is the corner of the square that fewer tourists get to.

A one-stop shopping alternative (but touristy...):

Lastly, and for shopping-guide thoroughness, I'm going to tell you the name of a very big store near Santa Croce that has a large selection of jackets. BUT, this insert is an anomaly in this guide because this is not a store for locals, but a store where mostly only tourists go. However, you might like it if you want to do 'one-stop-shopping' as it has a large selection of 'a-cut-above' jackets (and other leather goods such as bags, wallets, etc.).

Peruzzi
where via dell'Anguillara, 5 (just off p. Santa Croce)
phone 055 28 90 39
store hours 9 - 7

www.peruzzispa.com

Leather Belts

There's only one store in Florence that deals exclusively in belts:

Marcus
where Borgo San Lorenzo, 29r (near Duomo)
store hours 9.30 – 7.30 Mon opens 3:30
phone   055 21 60 83

Patrizia and Marco have been working in the small niche of belt production for over 25 years and they really know their stuff. All belts are made in the Florence area following the Italian leather working tradition. The selection is extremely vast for both men and women: traditional calfskin, patent leather, snake skin, nappa, etc.   There is also a huge choice of buckles from classic looks in solid brass to elaborate worked metal with rhinestone embellishments.   Belts can be made-to-order, re-sized, and adapted right in the store. Prices from 10€ to over €100.

Leather Gloves

Like so many leather items in Florence, there's no shortage of gloves. Basically you can find them all over the place with prices ranging from €10 a pair to €100. If you just want a knock-around pair of gloves the market stalls are your best bet with prices starting at around €10.

If you want to go one level higher, there are several stores that offer good middle-range stuff. The stores in via Calzaiuoli or via Por Santa Maria will do (there are a couple in each road).

But, the thing about gloves is even if you get a super-high quality pair, you're still not going to break the bank since gloves are small items and even the best can be bought for well under €100. Two shops worth visiting to buy a really nice pair of gloves are:

Madova (since 1919)
where via Guicciardini, 1r (near Ponte Vecchio)
store hours 9:30 – 7:30 (closed on Sundays)
phone 055 23 96 526

Madova is the first name in gloves in Florence. This is the only shop in town dedicated exclusively to their own production and selling of leather gloves (this is a 4th generation family-run business). The shop offers top-notch leather craftsmanship at competitive prices (from €40 up). Vast selection for men and women.

www.madova.com

Sermoneta Gloves
where via della Vigna Nuova, 28r
store hours 9:30 – 7:30 (closed on Sundays)
phone 055 23 96 526

A Roman glove manufacturer which, in addition to the more classic styles, produces also some extravagant looks. Worth checking out if you want out-of-the-ordinary gloves for some special occasion (lace, embroidered, cashmere, leopard pattern, etc).

www.sermonetagloves.com

Hand Made Goods

Ceramics

There are many ceramics workshops in and around Florence which produce the ceramics you see all over town (ceramics from the Umbrian city of Deruta are also popular).

Typical Florentine designs usually involve images of the countryside, grapes, leaves and Tuscan nature scenes. Yellow is a predominant color, reminiscent of the sunflowers spotted all over the Tuscan hills.

Common items are serving platters and large-size dishes and bowls, for use or for decorative purposes. Also pitchers and espresso coffee sets are popular as well as smaller items such as ash trays and spoon rests.

The shops listed below sell ceramics that are guaranteed made-in-Italy and hand painted.

A. Carnesecchi
where via Guicciardini, 4r (between Pitti Palace and Ponte Vecchio)
store hours 10 - 7
phone 055 23 98 523

This shop is right in the heart of Florence, on probably one of the busiest streets in town. What sets 'Carnesecchi' apart from all the other shops in the downtown area? Firstly, several of the hand-painted designs and patterns are exclusive to the shop and can't be found elsewhere in Florence. Then, Matteo and Lucy take special care of their customers. Ask them to personalize a ceramic piece and they will have it done for you within a day or two (eg. have a Christmas ornament customized or a magnificent hot plate in a Florentine geometric pattern with your family name added).

The shop also has some replicas of Della Robbia terra cotta pieces as seen in the Bargello museum as well as reproductions of other Renaissance works. For the real ceramics aficionado. Small items from €6, large decorative wall platters up to €300.

Ditta Luca della Robbia (since **1904**)
where via del Proconsolo, 19r (near Bargello museum)
store hours 10 − 6:30   Mon and Sun 2 − 6:30
phone 055 28 35 32

A long-standing ceramics shop in Florence. The shop is right outside the Bargello museum, and as the store name implies, you can find many Della Robbia reproductions in the well-known white and sky-blue colors as well as other pieces that can be seen in the Bargello. A large selection of De Ruta ceramics as well.

Ceramiche Rampini
where via Borgo Ognissanti, 32 (near p. Ognissanti)
store hours Mon - Sat 10 − 7
phone 055 21 97 20

The Rampini family have been making ceramics for three generations. This is not a shop but a large store. They have enormous variety and the ceramics are truly top-of-the line. You aren't likely to find ceramics with more ornate details, more intricate designs, or richer colors than these. Many pieces are inspired by Florentine traditions such as the giglio, the Medici coat-of-arms, and historic frescoes, but, of course, there's also the Tuscan countryside and nature scenes in general. *Visit their website for a very informative look at how ceramics are made step-by-step.*

Prices: higher than most other shops in town as the superior quality and intricacy of designs would dictate, small pieces however go for under €50.

www.rampiniceramics.com

Ceramics shops that are also workshops

The shops listed below are owned by the artisans who produce all the items in the store workshop. Buying directly from the person who actually made the piece you purchase leaves you with a real sense of authenticity. It should be said however that since these shops only sell what the individual owners produce, they don't carry as large a selection as the shops listed above and have less variety of styles.

Limbo
where via Dante Alighieri, 12r (near piazza Signoria, parallel to via del Corso)
store hours Mon - Sat 9:30 - 1:30 & 2:30 - 7
phone 055 26 45 241

This is a ceramics workshop but also an art gallery with paintings and etchings. There is a small selection of lovely ceramic pieces which are very different in design to the majority of items found in Florence. These works are inspired not by the Tuscan countryside and Florentine images but by traditions of Renaissance ceramic designs (a popular image is the colorful eye-spotted tail of the peacock). There are replicas of pieces found in the Bargello museum and De Ruta inspired items. Platters in the €60 range, mugs about €18.

Le Mie Ceramiche (since **1999**)
where via Verdi, 8r (just off piazza Santa Croce)
store hours Mon- Sat 9:30 – 1:30 & 2:30 - 7
phone 055 24 66 007

Ambra, the ceramics artist, produces pieces that remind you of the Tuscan countryside and Florence in general. In her shop you can see some of the ceramics before they've been put in the oven for baking (it's interesting to see how different they look at this mid-way point).   Small bowls around €25, mugs about €20.

www.facebook.com/lemieceramiche

Florentine Mosaics

The first workshop dedicated to the art of Florentine mosaics was set up in Florence in 1588 by the Medici. Florentine mosaics are made by putting pieces of semi-precious stone together to form an image. Differently from other types of mosaic styles, the colored pieces are joined so closely that you can't tell that the final 'picture' is made up of hundreds of pieces of stone.

The finished product is indeed a work of art – buying one of these pieces is akin to buying a valuable painting. Mosaic 'paintings' usually depict flowers, animals or nature scenes, but mosaics are also used to create table-tops and as ornamentation in wood cabinets.

Unfortunately, today this is becoming a dying art as it requires enormous patience and skill and years of training. There are however a few artists in Florence who continue the tradition. In order to understand the specialized nature of this craft, I recommend that you visit one of these workshops.

Workshops which sell their own productions

Le Pietre nell'Arte
where via Ricasoli 59R (between piazza Duomo and piazza San Marco)
store hours   9:30 – 6:30
phone   055 21 25 87

This is the most central workshop and is closest to the 'Opificio' museum dedicated to Florentine mosaics. In the gallery you can see a demonstration of how mosaics are made. Either the artist is working on a piece or the shop-assistant has a small work area where demonstrations are carried out (you might have to ask to be shown if a demonstration is not underway).

www.scarpellimosaici.it

I Mosaici di Lastrucci
where via dei Macci, 9
store hours 9 – 1 & 3 – 7
phone 055 24 16 53

Slightly off the beaten path from where most tourists pass, in this very large workshop you can see it all: how mosaics are made, mosaic 'paintings', cabinets, table-tops, and more. A wonderful place to understand mosaics.

www.imosaicidilastrucci.it

Pitti Mosaici
Where Piazza Pitti 23R (and v. Guicciardini 60r)
store hours 10 – 1 & 3 – 7
phone 055 28 21 27

The workshop is not right in view, but around the corner so you won't see the artisans at work unless you ask the shop-assistant to show you. Pitti does a lot of work with mosaics used for interior design. See the photo books in the shop with pictures of the splendid homes they have helped create.

www.pittimosaici.com

Other retailers which carry mosaic pictures

Art Store Michelangelo, via Ricasoli 61r, tel. 055 28 82 59
Francesco Tei, Lungarno Acciaiuoli 44, tel. 055 21 70 86

see *www.florencewebguide.com/florentine-mosaics.html* for more
on Florentine mosaics

Artistic Glass

Florence isn't known for its glass-making traditions, but there are a few specialized shops in town.

Artigianni
where via Pisana, 98r (not far from Porta San Frediano)
store hours Mon 3:30 – 7:30, Tue – Sat 10 – 1 & 3:30 – 7:30
phone   cell. 393 40 78 282

Giovanni is a stained glass craftsman whose workshop is a joy to behold. In a burst of iridescent colors and creative designs, you can find small items, such as pocket-mirrors and photo frames, and large pieces like wall mirrors or lamps. Prices are very fair. *Via Pisana is also a quaint street that is untainted for the most part by tourism, very worth strolling down, from Porta San Frediano to the delicious pastry shop 2 blocks down from 'Artigianni'.*

fb. artigianni

La Bottega dei Cristalli
where via dei Benci, 51r
store hours 10 – 7:30   **phone**   055 23 44 891

This is the best shop in Florence for small items made out of Murano glass. These pieces are all 100% Venetian, there are no fakes here. Browsing in this shop will surely put you in a good mood, there's so much colorful and ingenious stuff. Necklaces, earrings, bracelets, candies and fruit, bowls, glasses, frames, cuff links, pendants, bottle stoppers, the list is endless. Prices are very reasonable.

www.labottegadeicristalli.com

Galletti Shop
where via Borgo Ognissanti, 62r
store hours 9 – 1 and 3 – 7   Sun closed
phone 055 23 98 446

This shop doesn't deal solely in Venetian glass, but it does have a nice selection of Murano pieces. If you can't get to the 'Bottega dei Cristalli', this would be a viable alternative.

www.gallettishop.com

Seguso Archimede
where via dei Rondinelli, 3r (near p. Antinori)
store hours 10 – 7   Mon opens at 11   Sun closed
phone 055 28 34 67

Artistic glass doesn't get any better than this. The glass statuettes, vases, lamp fixtures, and home furnishings found in this Venetian based store are in a class by themselves. The subtlety of the colors, hue-blending and special effects (eg air bubbles or glitter within the glass) that Seguso can achieve is a rarity indeed. Prices are in the top range.

www.aseguso.com

Florentine Paper

The production of Florentine paper is a local craft that goes back centuries.

Originally paper was used as an inexpensive substitute for more prestigious decorative materials such as silk, leather, or wood to decorate walls, household objects, or even as a replacement for (much more expensive) glass in windows.

In order to beautify their surroundings, people developed the art of paper decoration.

Florentine paper is distinguished by its use of the 'giglio', the Florence lily flower, in its stamped patterns, along with other intricate floral designs. The paper is usually in earthy colors, dark greens, golds or bricky reds, and with a very dense pattern and little blank space.

Another very popular style of Florence paper is 'marbleized' paper which has patterns resembling the colored veins of marble.

The paper is sold in large sheets and can be used as gift wrapping, drawer or shelf lining, book covers or other uses. Florence paper patterns are also used to make stationery, cards, notepads, agendas and other writing and desk supplies.

Florence is full of street vendors selling factory produced stationery items in Florentine paper style.

However, hand-crafted goods with original designs can be found in specialty stores called 'cartoleria'.

Il Cartiglio (since 1980)
where via del Proconsolo, 63r (just behind piazza Duomo)
store hours Tue – Sat 9:30 – 1 and 2:30 – 7 (Mon opens 10:30, Sun only 2:30 – 7)
phone 055 28 43 41

This is a family run Florentine paper shop. Every item in the store is made by the artisans who own the boutique. In the morning you can see Francesca, the third generation of paper makers, producing the picture frames, agendas, book covers, and other items in the store (see a very down-to-earth and informative video of Francesca at work on the store website).

An especially beautiful article which is exclusive to 'il Cartiglio' is a particular leather binding used for books, photo albums and similar items. This leather has been heat-pressed with a very rich floral pattern creating a delicate and refined effect.

Since all products are produced by the shop itself, it's no problem making personal requests for custom-made items, and prices are a bit lower than other paper stores.

Gift ideas start at €10 or less.

www.ilcartigliofirenze.it

Il Papiro (since 1976)
where via Guicciardini, 47r (between Pitti Palace and Ponte Vecchio)
store hours 10 – 7:30 (Sun closes at 7)
phone 055 27 76 351

Il Papiro specializes in paper and stationery items all in the Florentine style. See a demonstration in the shop of how the 'marble paper' is created – this is real treat. Everything in the store is hand made in the Papiro workshop in the Florence area (writing paper, greeting cards, bookcovers, place cards, desk paraphernalia, etc.) It's very hard to come out of this shop empty handed.

Gift ideas start at €10 or less.

Il Papiro also offers lessons on book binding and 'marbling' of paper in the workshop in Grassina, near Florence. €50 a person. For information: *sonia@ilpapirofirenze.it*

www.ilpapirofirenze.it

Additional Papiro shops in the downtown area:
Via Cavour, 49r
Via de' Tavolini, 13r
Piazza del Duomo, 24r
Lungarno Acciaiuoli, 42r
Via Porta Rossa, 76r
Via Guelfa, 46r

Giulio Giannini & Figlio (since **1856**)
where Piazza Pitti, 37r (in front of Pitti Palace)
store hours 10 – 7 (Sun 11 – 6:30)
phone 055 21 26 21

This historical shop specializing in Florentine paper and leather book binding goes back to Florence's 'Victorian' era. In the late-1800's Florence had a large English population who were for the most part quite well-to-do. Giulio Giannini perfected the art of paper and leather decoration for his British clientele who had a great appreciation of such detailed and creative Florentine craftsmanship.

Admire Giannini's leather book bindings, Florentine paper desk sets, photo albums (perfect as wedding albums), greeting cards, writing paper, and endless other stationery items decorated with the exclusive Giannini stamp patterns.

The shop's ambience is also wonderful as both the façade and interior have been pretty much maintained as they were over 100 years ago.

www.giuliogiannini.it

Linens and hand-embroidery

Delicately embroidered linens for the home as well as lingerie and sleepwear are highly valued items in Florence. The four shops listed below are all specialists in this craft but each offer quite different goods.

Loretta Caponi
where piazza degli Antinori, 4r
store hours 9 – 1 and 3:30 – 7:30 (Sun closed)
phone 055 21 10 74

Here's a bit of trivia: Lady Diana had her wedding trousseau made in this shop. That must give you an idea of the level we're talking here. The bed linens, tablecloth sets, nightgowns, and lingerie are of unparalleled elegance. The shop too is impressive with frescoed arched ceilings and antique decor.

Prices are very high (eg hand-embroidered nightgown €400). There's a section for children's clothes (near the 'via delle Belle Donne' entrance) with gorgeous dresses for €100 – 200.

www.lorettacaponi.it

Le Telerie Toscane ('Tuscan linens')
where Sdrucciolo de' Pitti, 15r (right off piazza Pitti)
store hours 10:30 – 1:30 and 2:30 – 6:30 (Sun & Mon closed)
phone 055 21 61 77

Giulia learnt the craft of embroidery by working for the best embroideress in Florence, Loretta Caponi (see above). She then set off on her own, aimed at combining a traditional craft with modern day tastes and needs. Here the focus in on linens for the home (tablecloth and napkin sets, runners, underplates, dishtowels, etc) and the selection offers a wide assortment of colors, styles, embroidery and patterns. Items here are very modern and practical.

www.letelerietoscane.com

Grazia Giachi
where via Borgo Ognissanti, 6r (near p. Goldoni)
store hours 10 – 1:30 and 2:30 – 7 (Sun & Mon closed)
phone 055 28 50 64

White is the color here. The majority of articles in this shop are white with white embroidery. If you like this delicate very feminine look, go here. In this boutique the preference is on lingerie and nightgowns rather than linens for the home, cotton is used more than other materials, and prices are very fair (eg €80 hand-embroidered nightgown).

www.graziagiachi.it

TAF
where via Por San Maria, 17r (at 22r, children's clothes)
store hours 10 – 19 (Sun opens at 11)
phone 055 23 96 037

This shop looks old-fashioned as it goes back to 1954. The linens too are very traditional designs and styles. Emphasis on linens for the home and clothes for babies and children (for religious services, christenings, etc). Lovely gift sets at very reasonable prices.

www.tafricami.com

Jewelry

Gold

Florence has some of the country's best goldsmiths and of course the gold-dealers on the Ponte Vecchio are world famous. Objectively speaking, the quality of gold jewelry in Italy is very high.

Bear in mind that Italian gold is 18 carat, not 10k or 14k as you often find outside of Italy (you may find 10 and 14k in Florence, but it's there mostly for non-locals). 18k gold costs more, but is more valuable, softer and a deeper color. BTW, since 18k gold is 75% gold and 25% other metal, it's written as '750' in Italy (not 18k), so that's what you need to look for if you want to check for authenticity.

Buying jewelry is a highly personal choice since 'beauty is in the eye of the beholder'; only you can decide what you like and how much it is worth paying for. However, a useful thing to know is the market price for gold. You can easily Google it to find out (a useful site is also: www.goldpricenetwork.com).

At the time of this writing the market rate was **€28** per gram for 18k gold. However, you have to also consider mark-up costs for retail margins such as marketing costs, store overhead and the costs of labor for actually turning the gold into a piece of jewelry.

So, with that in mind, I decided to carry out some research for this guide.

I went around to shops in all different areas: on the Ponte Vecchio and surrounding streets, shops in other touristy areas and then shops in neighborhoods where tourists rarely go shopping. I asked for the same article in all shops: an 18k gold link chain bracelet of medium width (about 8 grams).

For each price I was quoted, I divided the price by the weight of the bracelet. This gave me the price the store was charging per gram so I could see which stores had the most competitive prices. I saw that retail prices start at double the market rate (but that's a very good price) and go up to 3, 4, or even 5 times more.

One rule of thumb is: the heavier the piece, the less you pay per gram. I actually found this to be true. Most of the bracelets I was pricing were 6-8 grams and the range in prices per gram went from **€60 – 150**, whereas the 3 times I was offered a heavier bracelet (14-15 grams) the price went down to around **€50-55** per gram in all 3 instances.

I was not surprised to find that some of the highest prices were on the Ponte Vecchio. But, it must be said that rent for shops on the 'Old Bridge' is exorbitant, so a mark-up has to be expected. However, some shops are really extreme in their mark up.

It's true though that some people are particularly keen to buy from a shop on the bridge, and to know that their piece is 'from the Ponte Vecchio'. If this is you, don't despair. Some shops there have prices that are very fair (see addresses below).

Interestingly – and this may serve as a warning to you potential customers – most stores were quick to weigh the piece for me, as weight has always been a criteria for pricing gold (even though more than one gold-dealer explained that nowadays prices are not based solely on weight but on the amount of work needed to produce a piece).

However, there were some stores which did not want to weigh the gold (some didn't even have a scale in the store and had to borrow one!), and these turned out to be the shops which had the highest prices (**110 and 150** euros per gram).

So, even though weight may no longer be the only criteria, a professional gold-dealer will readily provide you with the weight of a piece – beware of those who say it 'isn't their policy'.

Another thing I want to mention is that there is a 'game' that seems to be very common. The shop quotes a price for a piece, and then says 'but that's the price BEFORE the discount, let me see what it comes to AFTER the discount...' , then they start punching at the calculator and say 'so the final price is ....'.

This gimmick makes customers feel that they are getting a deal. Yet, there are shops that don't put on this 'show' and their prices can be just as low, or lower, than the 'final price' of these 'discounter' shops.

I'm not saying that you might not get a decent final price at these shops, but once you know about this trick I think you'll be better able to comparison shop.

The bottom line should be the price per gram if you want to compare prices from one shop to another for a similar piece of jewelry.

From my comparison shopping, I saw that the majority of shops were selling gold jewelry at between **75 to 85** euros per gram, so about 2.5-3 times the current market quote of **€28** per gram.

The best rates I found were about **€60** per gram, about double the market-price, at the following retailers.

1) Caselli (since **1980**)
where via Por S. Maria, 24r (street leading up to Ponte Vecchio)
store hours 9:30 – 7:30 Sunday closed
phone 055 23 96 281

A lovely small jewelry boutique that is unassuming and simple – no air of 'Tourist Trap' at all. Brother and sister run the shop and are pleasant, helpful and professional. With very little fanfare (no pulling out of calculator to tell me about the great discount I was going to get….), I was quoted **€60** per gram for a very pretty 18k gold link bracelet – the lowest rate I'd found.

2) Vaggi (since **1965**)
where Ponte Vecchio, 2/6r
store hours 9:30 – 7   Sun 10 - 6
phone 055 21 55 02

The Vaggi family have 2 boutiques on the bridge (this is a third generation family run shop). Here too I was quoted the low rate of **€60** for a nice 18k gold link chain (again, straightforward simple quote, no 'discount'). The service here was very professional and pleasant. My friend bought an antique style pendant here and was thoroughly satisfied with the professional service and fair prices. Shop has a very large selection of pieces, from simple to elaborate. Vaggi are also retailers of the prestigious 'Buccellati' brand of jewelry, famous for its lacework design with stones. The back section of the store is dedicated to these unique pieces.

www.vaggi.it

Also on Ponte Vecchio:
- **Piero Fallaci**, Ponte Vecchio 43r, tel. 055 29 44 65, a small shop, I was quoted **€67** per gram.

3) Romano
where via Cerretani, 35-39r (the final part of the street heading from station to Duomo)
store hours 9 – 7, Sunday closed
phone 055 21 10 48

On the extremely busy street where it's located, Romano is a bit of a hidden shop since it's downstairs in a basement location. This store has an authentic feel and I can easily see locals coming here (indeed I think most tourists would walk right passed it). They had a good selection of chain bracelets and provided attentive and professional service. I was quoted **€63** per gram. Has a large selection of watches.

4) Fabiani
where Piazza della Stazione, 23r (on side of station where escalators are)
store hours 9 – 7
phone 055 21 36 34

Fabiani is a large-scale retail store for jewelry. It does not have a boutique feel, but it offers a large selection of all varieties of gold (10k, 14k, 18k, etc) and has various price ranges. You won't find particularly unique pieces here, but If you are in the market for standard stuff (eg a chain, hoop earrings, etc.), this shop is good. The regular prices are in the **€75 – 85** per gram range, BUT they often have sales on certain styles and types of gold jewelry. The day I went I was quoted **€50** per gram for 2 bracelets. That's easily an unbeatable rate for 18k Italian gold in downtown Florence. The sale items are in display cases with the % off clearly marked.

Goldsmith artisans

These are some goldsmiths sell their own work which they produce in their workshop/shop.

Oro due
where via Lambertesca, 12r (nearish Ponte Vecchio)
store hours Mon 3:30 – 7, Tue – Sat 9:30 - 7   (Sun closed)
phone 055 29 21 43

Oro Due is a wonderful jewelry shop for anyone who is looking for something original and hand-made by a local goldsmith. This is a family-run artisan workshop and shop (the work area is in a back room in the store) where father, son and daughter make creative jewelry in gold but also silver and other materials.

Florentine and renaissance styles are one of the shop's special niches. They have what's called 'hammered-gold' – a Florentine way of working gold to give an antique effect that is very unique.

The service here is personalized and professional and very friendly too – I really recommend checking out their **Florentine style pieces** such as **Florentine ring bands,** and items inspired by the symbols of Florence such as the *giglio* lily and the *fiorino* coin.

Prices: Oro Due has **very fair prices** with something for all pockets, including pieces of their most popular items re-done in silver which are less expensive

Alessandro Dari
where via San Niccolò, 115r (cross Ponte Vecchio, turn left, 10 minute walk)
store hours 10 – 7:30, Sun closed in morning
phone 055 24 47 47

The only gold workshop that's also a museum (free entry). Dari's pieces are majestic, artistic and historical. You might find a cupola on top of a ring or even a Renaissance castle. Top range prices.

www.alessandrodari.com

Costume Jewelry

Florence is full of shops where craftspeople make and sell costume jewelry. You can find necklaces, bracelets and earrings made with less-valuable metals or metal alloys and adorned with beads, synthetic stones, crystals, or plastic. Other jewelry makers use yarn, felt, wood, ceramics, or even paper-mache.

Since preferences in costume jewelry are so personal it's hard to make a recommendation for one shop or another. It won't be a problem to find the shops, they're all over, and prices are quite similar from one shop to the next.

A few stores however set themselves apart:

Artigianato Anny (since **1984**)
where via dei Cerchi, 4r (parallel to via Calzaiuoli)
store hours 10:30 – 7:30   **phone** 055 29 32 52

Longevity is a strong indicator of quality. In a city where costume jewelry shops open and close at the bat of an eye, this shop has been around for over 25 years. A family business, Dario Masi and his son make all the jewelry. Basically there are two styles. The majority are metal based pieces of brass, copper, silver, and bronze mixes made into wide bracelets, long flat earrings or flat necklaces. The other type is rhinestone and Swarovski crystal pieces such as glittering rings, pendants and brooches. Very reasonable prices in the €20 – 40 range.

Angela Caputi (since **1975**)
where via Santo Spirito, 58r (parallel to Lungarno Guicciardini)
store hours 10 – 1 and 3:30 – 7:30   Sun closed
phone 055 21 29 72

A Florentine high-fashion costume jewelry maker. Angela Caputi's designs keep winning awards and recognition on a national and international level (her work has even been displayed at New York's Metropolitan Museum). Her jewelry is made of synthetic materials such as plastic and special resins that are molded into unique textures and shapes in bright distinctive colors. The Caputi look is unmistakable: large, chunky, modern and chic with an ethnic undercurrent. Prices are surprisingly reasonable. **Second shop in Borgo SS Apostoli, 44 (near p. Santa Trinità).**

www.angelacaputi.com

Jean André
where via Guerrazzi, 43-47 (**off the beaten path,** east of piazza Donatello)
store hours Mon – Fri 10 – 1 and 3 – 6
phone 055 57 00 83

This is a large-scale costume jewelry maker and wholesaler with 35 years' experience. It's not a proper store per se and you would probably not notice it if you were just walking down the street. There are 2 spaces – both in a basement area – one very large space where the jewelry is made and a small shop on the left where they sell to the public. Jean André is a supplier to important Italian and foreign department stores (eg Rinascente).

The costume jewelry at Jean André is a bit higher-scale than most Florence boutique offerings. These pieces would look just great as a complement to evening dresses or stylish skirt suits, even at formal occasions. There's also plenty of very pretty pieces for every day use. Pieces are made of faux coral, amethyst, rubies, jade and other stones, Swarovski crystals, cubic zirconia, faux pearls and mother-of-pearl.

Prices: prices are not always written on the goods — if the jewelry has been tagged to be sent to one of the store's retailers, it has a price which gets sold at approximately 50% less. Otherwise it depends on the piece but a general idea is €10 earrings, €20 necklaces.

Getting there: short taxi ride or 10 minute bus ride. Take bus no. 13 direction 'David' — if you get on at the station this is the first stop. The bus stop is on the pharmacy side of the station, go past the escalators as if you're walking away from the station but don't cross the street, before you get to the large roundabout, there's the bus stop for no. 13 called 'Stazione Parcheggio' (near the car ramp to the underground garage). Get off at 'Della Robbia 3' stop, walk to the corner and turn left into via Farina, walk straight and the next left is via Guerrazzi.

Luxury costume jewelry:

Alcozer & J
where via Porta Rossa, 14r (near Porcellino market)
store hours 10:30 – 2 and 3 – 7:30
phone 055 28 96 88

Alcozer's pieces are inspired by the past and in particular Renaissance style jewelry with a modern interpretation. Each piece is a mini work of art, hand-crafted using a metal fusion base and then embellished with semi-precious stones, crystals or pearls. High-end prices.

www.alcozer.it

Supplies for do-it-yourselfers:

For those who enjoy making costume jewelry themselves, there are three suppliers of all sorts of materials to make your own creations:

Fuxia, via Cavour 65 a/r, tel. 055 21 58 60

www.fuxiafirenze.com

Kix, via San Gallo 83r, tel. 055 48 98 97

Babilà, via Pisana 48r (across the Arno river, near Porta San Frediano), tel. 055 22 86 465

Clothes & Accessories

Italian fashion is world famous and Florence has no lack of wonderful clothing shops. This is the longest section of this shopping guide because there is so much variety available in town. This section is divided into several parts for easier reading.

For the most part I only include Italian stores which sell made-in-Italy articles (there are some exceptions which are noted). Sure, there's a Zara and an H&M store in Florence, but since these are not Italian brands, they are not included in this guide.

I'm assuming that people who want to shop in Italy would prefer to purchase authentic Italian made items.

Some Important Shopping Streets

Street: via Panzani - via de' Cerretani

This is the street that everyone has to walk down as it leads from the train station to the cathedral, the Duomo. Coming from the station, it starts as via Panzani, in the middle (where it makes a slight curve) it becomes via de' Cerretani.

It's loaded with stores (and people), many of which sell clothes that are quite reasonably priced in spite of the fact that this might seem like a very touristy block.

Some shops that are popular with locals are (in order walking from station to Duomo):

Blue Sand
where via Panzani, 34r
store hours 10 – 8, Sun 10:30 – 1 & 2 – 7:30

The stuff here fits great — they have lots of styles that look good on all body-types. The style is sporty/playful and in touch with the latest trends. The clothes are also very comfortable with prices from €20 – 40.

www.bluesand.it

Promod
where via dei Cerretani, 46
phone 055 21 78 44
store hours Mon – Sat 10 – 8, Sun 11 – 8

A large majority of the clothes here are not made-in-Italy, but I include this store because it is extremely popular with Florentines. They have very low prices, a huge selection of fashionable clothes and great service. At Promod you can find colorful bright clothes, frilly adorned looks, as well as a more sober classic look. The store is very big and is always busy which gives it a 'department store feel' in that you can get lost in all the selection and can stroll around for hours without being noticed - good if you like un-disturbed shopping.

www.promod.it

Milo
where via Panzani, 37r
store hours 10 – 7:40

Milo has 'jazzy' fun clothes, costume jewelry, a small selection of shoes, coats, hats, belts. If you're looking for something for a party or just clothes with a bit more flair this is the place. Jeans with rhinestones, jackets with fur trimming, blouses with frilly collars, belts with extravagant beaded buckles, etc. The clothes are very girly and fun yet stylish for adult women too. Reasonable prices.

The End
where via Cerretani, 5-9r
phone 055 21 27 85
store hours 10 – 8 (Sundays 12 – 7)

One of my favorite shops. They have a great mix of clothes, from trendy or unconventional outfits to the classic jacket and pants suit. **Clothes for men and women.** Prices from €50 up.

Street: Borgo San Jacopo (across the Arno, cross Ponte Vecchio and turn right)

This is a street you might not go down in your Florentine wanderings since most people, after crossing the Ponte Vecchio, just go straight since the continuing street takes you to Pitti Palace. But this is a very good road for shopping. It's more peaceful (ie less crowds) and has more local flavor than most central streets and has a nice selection of different types of stores at various price ranges.

I recommend just wandering and popping in and out of shops (it's not a long road) but here's a list of some popular shops: **Cinzia** at 14r (hand-made hats), **Gabriella Gonnelli** at 44r (lovely top/skirt sets and very feminine clothes with artistic decorations), **Jasmine** at 27r (modern Italian brands for men & women: Pianura Studio and Versace Jeans), **Roberta** at 74r (nice leather bags under €100), **Glamour** at no. 49 (more mature styles, not a modern store but has classics at good prices).

Street: Via Tornabuoni

Via Tornabuoni and its surrounding streets (via della Vigna Nuova, via Strozzi, via dei Calzaiuoli) is where you go for exclusive labels. This is the main street for luxury brands and as you walk in this area you see one top designer store after another. All these famous name shops are listed in a separate chapter of this guide ('Designer Label Stores') where you will find opening hours, contact details and facts about the history of the designer.

Clothes for Men and Women

The first two stores below are listed separately because they are considered institutions in the Florentine shopping scene for clothes. They both have lots of selection in different styles for **men & women** and the prices are fair. 'Matucci' has younger styles and is a bit higher-end than 'Santini'.

Matucci
where via del Corso, 71r (street off v. dei Calzaiuoli)
store hours 10 – 7:30 (closed on Sun in July and August)
phone 055 23 96 420

This store is on 3 levels but still has a shop-like feel to it. A wonderful store that has a large selection of brand names in casual everyday styles as well as dressier looks. This shop has good quality and competitive prices with fairly traditional classic pieces that don't go out of style. This is what most people think of when they think of the real 'Italian' look. **Prices:** €100 and up

Santini
where via Alamanni, 35r (station area on the tram side)
store hours 9 – 1 and 4 – 8, Mon mornings closed, Sun closed but open during busy seasons
phone 055 29 31 32

A huge store which seems more like a wholesale outlet than a retail shop. The prices too. Santini has fairly conservative clothes at extremely reasonable prices, thanks to its 'no fanfare' approach. This is a no-nonsense shop for the sensible shopper who wants quality at a reasonable price and is not interested so much in the latest designer fad. Vast majority of clothes designed and made in Italy (look for label).   If you like the classic styles, go here.   Large choice of 'dressy' clothes for special occasions.

Price range: inexpensive (eg women's dresses starting at €35, jeans €30, shirts for men €35 etc.)

Women's Clothes

Under €80 range

Glam
where via fra' Bartolomeo, 13r (near piazza della Libertà)
store hours 9:30 – 7:30 (Sun closed)
phone 055 57 77 25   cell: 338 99 91 643

This store is slightly off the usual tourist path, but really it's just a 15 minute walk from piazza San Marco or a few minutes bus ride. Pucci, Gucci, Prada, Max Mara, Armani, Ferragamo, Miu Miu, and other designers can be found at Glam at a fraction of what you normally pay for these labels.

The shop has mostly clothing but there are also some bags, shoes and other accessories. These are items that are not 100% new (although you can hardly tell) and are being re-sold at much lower prices. Don't think 'second-hand store' — Glam lives up to its name! The shop also sells new garments by other Italian brands at extremely competitive prices. This is the only store I found in Florence where you can easily find designer labels for under €50.

By bus: no. 17 (direction 'Verga') to 'Fra' Bartolommeo 01 - Hotel San Gallo Palace' stop. If you get on in San Marco square in front of 'Pugi' bakery, you get off at the 2nd stop.

Walking: from piazza San Marco, at the right of the church, take via La Pira - which eventually becomes via Lamarmora - to the end, cross wide avenue, via fra' Bartolomeo is on other side.

Echo
where via del Oriuolo, 37r (near piazza del Duomo)
store hours 10 – 7:30 (Mon opens at 11, Sun 3:30 – 7:30)
phone 055 23 81 149

Feminine looks arranged in the shop by color. The front of the store has the more elegant clothes, the back room has the looser-fitting casual clothes. Lovely touches (embroidery, designs, lacy add-ons) that give clothes a special flair. Styles: more girl than woman.

www.echofirenze.it

Georgette
where gallery beneath train station – from bottom of escalators walk straight, store on right
store hours 10 – 7.30 (Sun closed)

Large-scale production allows for inexpensive prices for what I would call 'party clothes'. This is a good place to go to get an outfit for a special occasion (wedding, graduation party, etc) without spending a lot. Very feminine looks, lively colors, patterns with beads, rhinestones but also retrò styles as well as traditional suits and dresses.

Carries Italian 'Rinascimento' brand (*www.rinascimento.com* – the site is in Italian but you can see pictures of their clothes under the tab 'collezioni').

Dance
where Borgo Pinti, 48r (behind 'Pergola' theater)
store hours 10:30 – 7
phone cell: + 39 377 43 99 657

Don't be thrown off by the name, this is not a store for dance clothes. The store owner, Nicola Parisi — who designs all the clothes himself — named the shop after his wife who is a ballerina. The store has a huge selection of clothes that tend toward the more elegant and womanly style. Lots of evening dresses and skirt and top sets, floral patterns, and form fitting cuts. It's hard to describe though because the racks are so chock-a-block full. Fantastic prices considering the personal design and production and the fine quality. **Note: no credit cards accepted.**

Blunauta
where via del Pronconsolo, 69r (near p. Duomo)
store hours 10:30 — 7:30 (Mon opens at 3:30, Sun closed)
phone 055 21 24 60

You might not go into this store as it looks quite plain from the outside. This is a shop dedicated to garments in silk, wool, cotton and cashmere. Comfortable knit dresses and sweaters at great prices. **More mature styles.**

<u>€80 - €180 range</u>

Carpe Diem (since **1993**)
where via Ricasoli, 52r (between piazza San Marco and Duomo)
phone 055 29 22 81
store hours Tue — Sat 10 — 2 & 3 - 7 (Mon & Sun closed)

A shop for girls and women's clothes — clientele ranges from 25 to 60 years. Beautiful Italian designed and produced clothing with a very feminine flair. Chic and sophisticated or fun-spirited and breezy styles, yet all very practical and comfortable. The shop carries the Italian designer Moschino, and also 2 popular Italian brands: Almeria, famous for its Tuleté knits ($$) and Tensione In ($) which makes very flattering and unique garments at surprisingly affordable prices. The owner, Emanuela, is very helpful and friendly. Ask her to show you the huge selection of gorgeous Moschino scarves (kept in the drawers).

Le Bonille (since **1994**)
where via Tosinghi, 42r (near piazza della Repubblica)
phone 055 29 14 35
store hours 10 – 7 (Sun opens at 11)

Right in the heart of town, this shop may look like all the others but is worth going into. Le Bonille specializes in clothes meant to be both **comfortable and stylish** (they also carry **plus-sizes**). Looks that are a bit adventurous without being too 'out there' for most people to wear. This boutique has several Italian designers and some French and Spanish labels.

Macel (since **1982**)
where via Guicciardini, 128r (near Palazzo Pitti)
store hours 10 - 7:30
phone 055 28 73 55

Macel is a true boutique. You will find carefully selected items catering to the elegant and refined woman who seeks out and appreciates quality. The shop offers a 'total look': if there is a dress that you like, Macel will also have the bag, scarf or jacket to match.

Carolina, the shop owner, and her friendly assistants Barbara and Martina are helpful in putting it all together for you. If you want high quality Italian women's wear you will appreciate this store. Italian fashion at its best.

Macel has some simpler casual pieces, but most items are for the 30+ lady who likes a stylish, and very feminine look.

Men's clothes

Gutteridge
where via della Vigna Nuova, 36r
store hours Mon 3 – 7:30, Tue – Sat 10 – 7:30 (also last Sunday of the month)
phone 055 26 54 235

A former British tailor's shop (set up in 1878) which now has good quality Italian men's wear at reasonable prices. Located among some of the most prestigious and expensive stores in Florence, Gutteridge stands out for its 'stockhouse' feel and welcoming atmosphere. Some items may not be made-in-Italy but most are, so check the label. Especially good deals on suits, blazers, and trousers.

Chelazzi (since 1974)
where via Guicciardini, 8r (near Ponte Vecchio)
phone 055 23 98 667
store hours 10 – 7 (Sun 11:30 – 6)

A small shop for men's shirts, knitwear and ties. Quality materials (cotton, silk, Merino wool, cashmere) at affordable prices. Classic lines with an Italian touch. Beautiful pullovers in Merino wool or wool/cashmere mix in triple woven Zegna-Baruffa knit fabric.

Price range: shirts €50 – 85, sweaters €85 – 190, ties €10 -40.

www.chelazzi.net

Bernardo
where via Porta Rossa, 87r
store hours Mon 3 – 7:30 Tue - Sat 9:30 – 1:30 and 3 – 7:30
(busy season open Sundays too)
phone 055 28 33 33

A cozy boutique specializing in quality men's wear. Bernardo prides itself on the fine fabrics and tailoring of the Italian brands sold in the store. Higher-end prices are justified by the good value of having a classic garment that won't go out of style and will last for a long time. Also custom made shirts, choose your fabric in the store.

If you aren't familiar with these Italian brands it's worth checking out Bernardo. shirts: *Barba* from Naples, suit jackets: *Cantarelli* from Arezzo and *Lardini* from Ancona, knits in cashmere and Merino wool: *Brunello Cucinelli* from Perugia, trousers: famous *Incotex* brand from Venice, pioneers of 'smart casual' leg wear, jackets: *Moorer* from Verona, *Herno* from Maggiore lake area, ties and scarves: *Fiorio* from Milan.

Rossini
where via Martelli, 11 (near Duomo)
store hours 10.30 – 7:30
phone 055 23 96 923

From the outside this shop looks small, but it's quite large inside. Men can find a total look here: shoes, belts, undergarments, shirts, knitwear, suits, trousers, scarves, etc. All made-in-Italy clothes medium to medium-high quality/prices. Traditional style clothes with modern innovations. Some price examples: €129 leather shoes, €390 wool suit.

In-town Outlet Stores

Thousands of tourists flock to the outlet malls in the hills around Florence each year looking for designer clothes and bags at discount prices. A separate section of this guide is dedicated to these out-of-town outlet villages.

However, there are some outlet stores located right in town where you can find exclusive labels for less. So, if you don't feel like taking an out-of-town trip, pop into one of these shops if you're looking for designer name clothes.

Basement
where via del Trebbio, 10r (off p. Antinori)
store hours Mon 3 – 7 Tue – Sat 10 - 7
phone 055 23 81 527

This outlet has been selling designer labels for over 20 years but is not very well known even by locals as it's on a hidden-away side street. 'Basement' has designer clothes from the current year and not the past year like most outlet stores. Brands change all the time since even the owners don't know what designer collections they'll be able to get their hands on each season (last time I was there they had lots of 'Cavalli'). All items are organized by size in easy to browse-through racks. Save 40-50% off market prices. Store stocks many 'lesser-known' Italian brands that are however extremely popular with Italian women (although they may not be household names abroad). More stylish than trendy looks – more 'woman' than 'girl' styles.

Prices: €100 and up range.

Sotto Sotto
where via Pietrapiana, 67r (near piazza dei Ciompi)
store hours 9:30 – 7:30 (in summer closes from 1:30 – 3:30)
Mon and Sun opens at 3:30
phone 055 24 78 850

A new large outlet store which carries the most important and prestigious Italian designers. Since most of these designers also have retail stores in Florence on the glamorous shopping streets, they certainly don't want it to be advertised that their goods can be bought at an outlet store in town. For this reason, it is considered inappropriate to advertise the actual names of the labels that 'Sotto Sotto' carries. Suffice it to say, this store has all the 'Big Ones'.

Clothes for **men and women.**

Also a large selection of designer bags, shoes and accessories.

Prices: due to the high-level of the brands on offer prices are in the higher range – save however 50 – 60% compared to regular retail prices for the same pieces.

www.sottosotto.it

Lo stock di Max
where via Pietrapiana, 15r (near piazza dei Ciompi)
store hours 10 – 2 & 4 – 7.30 (closed Mon mornings and Sun)
phone 055 24 10 84

A very simple-looking store that has mostly Max Mara, Max & Co. Marella, and Pennyblack stock piled onto very crowded racks. Large selection of jeans including Dolce & Gabbana for €40. All pieces go for under €100 with the average between

€20 - 60. You can also find 'Simon's Shirts' a made-in-Italy brand specializing in shirts for €30 each.

Luisa Via Roma Contemporary
where via S. Pellico, 9 (near p. d'Azeglio)
store hours 10:30 – 7:30 (Sun closed)
phone 055 21 78 26

Have you read about 'Luisa Via Roma' under the 'Special Mention' section? Then you know that 'Luisa' is one of the most prestigious stores not only in all of Florence but in all of Italy. This is the exclusive outlet store for 'Luisa' where you can buy clothes and accessories from the previous season. For the most part, prices are very high since even at a 30% or 50% discount these articles still can go for €200-300 or more. However, I did find several pairs of jeans at around €100 and there were some summer tops for around €70 the last time I was there.

Clothes for **men & women.**

www.luisaviaroma.com

Oceano Moda Stockhouse
where via Alamanni, 23D (near tram side of station)
store hours 9:30 – 7:30 (not always open on Sun)
phone 055 26 08 394 cell: 338 58 01 825

This store couldn't be less impressive to look at. You see a very ordinary shop called 'OceanoModa' and the stockhouse is the store to the right. Inside the tiny space there are just racks with lots of designer name clothes (brands change all the time). Clothes carry the original price tag, then you have to ask what the 'real' price is, and there's certainly room to bargain. **Men & women.**

A little known fact about this store is the **designer bags.** You can find some of the biggest and most popular Italian labels for nearly half of the retail market price. But you have to know about it and ask the owner to show you what they've got at the moment (not all bags are on display on the shelves for security purposes).

Also: great buys on men's suits for €200 (eg Fendi, Ferré).

One Price
where via Borgo Ognissanti, 74r (street parallel to Lungarno that ends in p. Ognissanti)
store hours 10 – 1 & 4 - 7
phone 055 28 46 74

A less-heralded stock house that may offer some good finds – brands change all the time. Very large selection of men's clothes with tailored shirts from Naples, suits and jackets all at reasonable prices.
Men & women.

Fuoriserie
where corner of via del Sole and via del Moro (near p. Santa Maria Novella)
store hours Tue – Sat 9 – 1 & 4 – 7:30 (open all day Sat in winter)
phone 055 23 82 638

If you didn't know about it you'd probably walk right by this store: it looks plain and old. Actually it's a stock house of the very popular 'Principe' store ('Principe' has its own brand and also carries several high-end labels). You can find some great deals on designer brands if you have the patience to wade through all the racks and shelves and you aren't put off by the non-glamorous atmosphere. **Men & women.**

Also a small room with a €5 – 10 euro rack and a **kids section with items from €5 – 30**.

Sonya boutique (since **1987**)
where Lungarno Acciaiuoli, 24r
store hours 9:30 – 7:30 (Sun closed)
phone 055 23 96 709

This boutique along the Arno carries the latest collections of Italian designers (Cavalli, Missoni, Ermanno Scervino, D. Exterior). It is not an outlet, but there is a great bargain room with 40-50% off on end-of-the-season pieces. Basically the whole back room is dedicated to this and you can find some really good discounts on top-designer clothes. Styles more woman than girl.

Clothes for full-figured women

In Italian larger-sizes are called 'taglie comode' (comfortable sizes) or 'taglie morbide' (soft sizes). Having generous curves does not mean sacrificing style though. Here's list of some of the shops downtown which cater to women with a full-figure.

Note: also **Le Bonille** (see above, under **'Women's Clothes'**) has excellent selection of plus-size clothes.

Appeal
where via Porta Rossa, 8r (off via Calzaiuoli)
store hours 10:30 – 7:30, Mon 2:30 – 7:30, Sun 11:30 – 7
phone 055 23 99 225

This is a lovely and very popular boutique for fashionable clothes in comfortable cuts and sizes. Most items are made of high-quality fabrics with only natural fibers. Claudia and Simona provide great service in helping to put together a flattering outfit. No tailored jackets or pants suits but free-fitting stylish pieces. Prices €90 and up.

fb: negozio Appeal

Nuova Lady
where via dei Tavolini, 21r (off via dei Calzaiuoli)
store hours 9:30 – 7 (closed from 1 – 2)
phone 055 21 55 67

A small boutique in the heart of town that has been in business for ages. Casual yet conservative styles for more mature women at very reasonable prices (€50 and up).

Nath Nath (since **1970's**)
where piazza N. Sauro, 4r (just over ponte Carraia)
store hours 9:30 — 1:30 and 3:30 — 7:30 (Sun closed)
phone 055 21 77 26

A small-scale Florentine chain store (other shop in via Gioberti, see 'Fringe Shopping' chapter) that has wonderfully comfortable clothes in fun bright patterns and designs. I especially love their viscose trousers that never wrinkle, feel silky and soft, fall just right, and don't need ironing (and hide bulges well). **Note:** not exclusively for plus-sizes, also caters to smaller fits. Prices €60 and up.

www.nathnath.it

Elena Mirò (since **1985**)
where via Tosinghi, 8r (near p. Repubblica)
store hours 10 — 7:30 (Sun opens at 11:30)
phone 055 26 57 725

This is a very large shop offering a wide selection of styles from everyday wear to dressier clothes. Tailored suits and jackets as well as knits — this store achieves the happy medium of 'smart casual', clothes that you can wear both to work or out for the evening. Good value.

www.elenamiro.com

Marina Rinaldi (since **1980**)
where via Panzani, 1r (street leading from station to Duomo)
store hours 10 — 2 and 3 — 7:30 (Sun opens at 11)
phone 055 23 82 343

Part of the world renowned Max Mara group, Marina Rinaldi specializes in fine women's wear in plus sizes. Rinaldi has several lines of garments (elegant, sporty, every day wear, etc.). Clothes here tend to have classic tailored designs. More popular with women aged 40+. Higher-end prices.

www.marinarinaldi.com

Concept Stores

Definition of a 'concept store': a shop that does not carry only one type of item but is meant to be an eclectic mix of original pieces which, as a whole, creates a unique shopping experience. When you enter a concept store you are meant to be in an 'explorer' mode, not coming in to look for one particular thing. For instance, a concept store might carry some clothes, some vintage shoes, hand-made jewelry, jazz cds and writing stationery all in one shop.

Florence's nicest concept stores:

Flo
where Lungarno Corsini, 30r (along Arno river)
store hours 10 – 7 (Mon opens at 3.30, Sun closed)
In summer: 9 – 1 & 4 – 8 (Mon morning and Sun closed)
Phone 055 53 70 568

A concept store selling clothes, bags and accessories made locally by Italian seamstresses and tailors. Pieces are often one-of-a-kind as the sewers make their garments from fabrics coming from a variety of sources and not in bulk (eg. recycling fabrics from vintage clothes, remnants from designer stock houses). Garments are a wonderfully varied mix of materials and styles. The boutique has lovely hand-crafted accessories: woven scarves in light linens, stylish hats, fun patterned leggings and tights, fashionable tote bags made from re-cycled designer scarves in silk – all made by local artisans and designers on a small-scale.

You may also find some vintage pieces as well as some bargains on new designer shoes or bags (eg Prada, Bottega Veneta).

There's also a lovely section with 100% environmentally friendly **children's clothes** called 'così come'è' and a second kids' line called 'tutti x uno' with button-on animal patches that can be changed according to pet preferences and color choice. Also hand-crocheted baby shoes.

Boutique Nadine
where Lungarno Acciaiuoli, 22r (near Ponte Vecchio) and via dei Benci 32r (near Santa Croce)
store hours Mon 2:30 – 7:30, Tue - Sat 10 – 7:30, Sun. 12 - 7
phone Lungarno Acciaioli 055 28 78 51- via dei Benci 055 24 78 274

This concept store has original ladies dresses, blouses, and skirts hand-made on a small-scale by local designers (the store's 'Odette' brand) as well as some vintage clothes and accessories. Also antique and antique-style jewelry and watches and several types of memorabilia, ornaments and vintage household items.

Note: both stores are similar, but the Lungarno store has a larger selection of vintage clothes, bags and shoes with many designer brands, the via dei Benci store has more collectible items and memorabilia.

www.boutiquenadine.com

Garbage' En
where via dei Cimatori 2r (near Dante's house)
store hours 10 – 7:30 (Sun closed)
phone 055 26 70 505

Two of the three ladies who opened this concept store are artists, and the three decided to put their minds together and create a line of clothes and accessories inspired by the city where they studied art and design: Florence. Their collections are a rich mix of modern colors and designs combined with the artisan craft of working leather. The shop has few pieces of each item which are hand-painted and locally made: bags, tops, belts, dresses, hats, accessories — the silk scarves are fabulous, ask the shop assistant to see them open so you can see the beautiful colors and designs. The shop feels a bit like a New York loft (albeit much smaller!).

www.garbageen.com

Urban chic fashion

These are shops that are considered at the fore-front of trendy contemporary city fashion. The clothes here are always a mix of labels combining mostly Italian, Japanese, British, American, Spanish, French and Scandinavian designers. The stores too are modern open-spaces inspired by metropolis living (eg a New York loft feel, a London underground look) – half the attraction of these shops is the atmosphere and ambience of the store itself.

Prices are for the most part high (ie most everything over a €100 going up to €300), especially considering that we're talking about clothes like cotton shirts or wool sweaters or a simple blazer, albeit made with the latest new type of cotton, or dyed in a very rare shade of blue or whatever, with some unique touch to set the clothes apart.

The majority of the customers in these stores are probably under 30 years old. This being said, all these shops also carry standard pieces that could suit anybody.

Just for curiosity's sake and to see this side of the Florentine shopping scene, I'd say a couple of these stores are worth popping into (especially the centrally located ones as these are streets you're bound to walk down or near anyway).

These stores have clothes, shoes and accessories for **men and women**.

Centrally located

Flow store
where via Vecchietti, 22r (near piazza della Repubblica)
store hours 10 – 7:30 (Sun & Mon opens at 3)
phone 055 21 55 04

A massive open space in a building from 1200. Aesthetically speaking, this store is beautiful to look at with its brick archways, high ceilings, wood floors and retro furnishings (at times the music is very loud though). An extremely varied mix of clothes and styles. Considered a very 'in' store.

There's a separate store for shoes right down the block in via Sassetti, 13r.

www.flow-store.it

Gerard loft
where via dei Pecori, 34r (near piazza San Giovanni)
store hours Tue – Sat 10 – 7:30, Sun - Mon 2:30 – 7:30
phone 055 28 24 91

Where the cool people shop – the majority of clothes here have a rugged look, and more guys shop here than girls. Just having a T-shirt with the name of this store across the front was considered the top in fashion sense a few years ago.

Many American and German labels some of which produce exclusive clothing lines sold only here.

www.gerardloft.com

Société Anonyme
where via Niccolini, 3f (near piazza D'Azeglio)
store hours Tue – Sat 10 – 7:30, Mon 3:30 – 7:30
phone 055 38 60 084

A very impressive place, both the store itself and what it sells (the shop shares its space with an architects' studio whose influence is strongly felt). This store has its own clothing line (avant-garde items) designed by the owner along with a long list of foreign and Italian labels. If you'd like to see what's in fashion at the moment in Berlin, Tokyo or Stockholm this is the place.

www.societeanonyme.it

Organic Clothes

Organic clothes are made out of materials that are cultivated under the standards of organic agriculture. This type of clothing is environmentally friendly as materials used have no chemicals.

There are three shops in Florence dedicated to organic fashion:

Giuditta Blandini – stile biologico
where Piazza Pitti, 6r
store hours 9 – 7, Sun 11 – 6 (summer: 9 – 1 & 4 – 7, Sun closed)
phone 055 27 76 275

This is Florence's (indeed, Italy's) first organic clothing boutique. Not only are all garments produced organically, they are also all hand-made. Most pieces come in white, beige or light colors and have a very refined delicate look.

Shop sells knitwear, shirts, skirts and dresses, but also vegetarian shoes, swimsuits and baby clothes. Most clothing for women but a small selection for men is also available.

Definitely worth checking out since shop is just in front of Pitti Palace, where most tourists go, so pop in while you're in the area.

Prices: average item between €90 – 140

www.stilebiologico.it

Alta Rosa
where via San Gallo, 84r (5 minute walk from piazza San Marco)
store hours Mon – Fri 9:30 – 1:30 & 2:30 – 7, Sat only morning
phone 055 46 25 190

This organic fashion boutique was founded by 2 architects and one clothing designer (all women, and the shop in fact sells only clothes for women). These ladies seek out the latest biologic materials and fabrics and design all the items in the store. White and light colors prevail and the style is delicate, loose-fitting, and comfortable.

Alta Rosa also has a special niche: wedding dresses (you can check these out on their website, 'abiti da sposa'). If the standard style of wedding dress just isn't 'you' and you would like to be more natural (but certainly elegant!) on your wedding day, give Alta Rosa a try.

Prices: average item between €100 – 160, also has a bargain rack €30 - 50

www.altarosa.it

Note: since this is such a small niche, for thoroughness I also include the entry below although most of the organic clothes at 'Campo di Canapa' are not made-in-Italy but are imported.

Campo di Canapa
where via G. Leopardi, 4r (near piazza della Beccaria)
store hours 9:30 – 7:30 Sun closed (in summer: 9:30 -1 & 3:30 – 7:30, Sat only morning)
phone 055 22 60 104

This is a no-frills earthy store that is right next to a vegetarian organic food shop/restaurant (considered by vegetarians to be the best in Florence).

The store sells clothes for men, women and children mostly all made of hemp (and some other organic materials). The majority of the articles are casual everyday wear in all styles and colors. The site has an online store so you can check out the collection and prices as well (€30 – 50 range).

By bus: from station take bus no. 14 (direction 'Ripa') or no. 23 (direction 'Sorgane' or 'Nave a Rovezzano') from the 'Valfonda' bus stop (leaving station on the pharmacy side, bus stop is on the left in a small square – you can see Burger King across the wide street in front). Get off at 'via Leopardi' stop – store right there.

www.insolititessuti.com

Dirt Cheap Clothes

These are some popular places where you can find Italian clothes at extremely inexpensive prices. For the most part the clothes are casual or sporty items.

Charget
where In the underground passageway of S.M.N. train station (in older part of passageway, in front of small hairdresser shop)
store hours Mon – Sat 10 – 7

You can recognize this tiny shop by looking for the store with no doors, it looks like the clothes are just spilling out onto the walkway. There are always racks of clothes outside the store too. It's packed with inexpensive ladies clothes, and is usually full of women too. **Price range**: items from €15.

Particolarissimo
where via Guicciardini, 57r (near Palazzo PItti)
store hours 11.30 – 7:30

This shop for casual clothes has a set price for every item in the store: **€19.90**. Loose, casual, comfortable clothes made in Italy. Some fancier pieces too. Only women's wear.

Alex
where via Faenza, 23r (near Medici Chapel)
store hours Mon – Sat 10 am – 7pm

Ladies wear, casual but not sporty. Loose fitting viscose and cotton items and dressier skirts and dresses, also pants and leggings. **Price range**: €15 – 30.

C C Magazine
where via della Stazione, 13/14r (near station)
store hours Mon – Sat 7:30 am – 8pm   **Sun** 10 – 8

Casual wear (ie cotton pullover shirts, tops, shorts, baggy summer pants, etc.) for men, women & children.   Also undergarments.   Made in Italy and imported clothes.   **Price range:** items from €5.

Melrose
where via Alamanni, 45r (near station)
store hours everyday 10 – 7

Some made in Italy items, others imported.   Casual sporty clothes but also some dressier items, especially for women, but store has clothes for men too. Price range: items from €10.

Streetwear

What is called 'streetwear' in Italy was originally clothes for the skateboard, surfing and snowboarding culture. Eventually this way of dressing became popular with the general public, and the demand for cool young-looking, active wear grew. This has evolved into the 'street' style that you don't have to be a teenager to wear.

Feedback store
where corso dei Tintori, 43r (nearish p. Santa Croce)
store hours Mon – Sat 10 – 8, Sun 2:30 – 7:30
phone 055 24 69 230

From the shop window this looks like just like a store for skateboarders – you probably wouldn't go in to look for clothes. But their stuff is great if you want an Italian twist on what could be called a 'rocker' look (think polished-up grunge). For instance, comfortable stretchy button-up shirts in colorful criss-cross patterns, very comfortable (riding) shorts with pockets that are perfect just for casual walking and everyday use, etc.

The shop carries four Italian labels whose clothes are all made by Italian streetwear artists. These items have some original touches that make what would normally be just a T-shirt or sweater something unique (eg. special silk-screening designs or pockets and zippers in original places). The shop assistant tells me their customers range from 15 – 65 years old (she herself is in her 40's and looks great in these clothes).

www.feedback-store.it

Children's clothes and maternity wear

Walking around downtown you'll see no shortage of high-quality children's clothes shops. Lower priced kids wear is harder to find, especially if you want something with a little more style. These shops are some of Florence's best kept secrets.

Sorelle Orlandi Cardini Kids
where via dei Servi, 79r (near piazza Santissima Anunziata)
store hours 10 – 7:30 (Sun closed)
phone 055 23 82 354

Any mother will fall in love with this store. They have such cute stuff for children, it's all hand-made, prices for clothes are so low (their most expensive item, a winter jacket, goes for €35).

fb: sorelle orlandi cardini

Ang
where via Gioberti 2dR (near piazza Alberti)
store hours Mon 3:30 - 7:30, Tue - Sat 9:30 - 2 & 3:30 - 7:30

Baby and children's clothes (0 - 10 years) all made by hand by the Italian owner, Agnese. Very playful, colorful, imaginative outfits for kids. All natural fibers and very soft biological cotton for sensitive skin. Dresses start at €20. Highly recommended.

By bus: No. 6 (direction 'Novelli'), get off at piazza Alberti stop.

www.angunbebe.com

Also the following shops have kids wear:
- **Flo** (see part **'Concept Stores'** above)
- **Fuoriserie** (see part **'In-town Outlet Stores'** above)

Luxury children's wear

Assunta Anichini (since **1912**)
where via del Parione, 59r
store hours 9:30 – 1:30 & 3:30 – 7:30, Mon only in pm, Sun closed
phone 055 28 49 77

This is the oldest children's clothing shop in Florence. Anichini sells high quality children's wear, christening and communion gowns, dressy outfits for special occasions all hand sewn and embroidered. High-end prices.

Some trivia: Michael Jackson had some clothes for his children made here when he came to Florence.

www.anichini.net

Baroni (since **1912**)
where via Porta Rossa, 56r
store hours Mon- Sat 9:30 - 7:30   Sun 11:30 – 7
phone 055 28 09 53

This Florentine store is still owned and run by the original Baroni family who has been producing clothes for children for three generations. Clothes, baby shoes and booties and accessories for children 0 -12. High-end prices.

www.baroni.com

Maternity Wear

Sarà (literally, 'it will be')
where via della Spada, 42r (near Marino Marini museum)
store hours 10 – 1 and 3:30 – 7:30   closed Mon morning and Sun
phone 055 28 10 48

Very flattering, feminine and elegant clothes for expectant moms. Everyday wear and fancier outfits all in stretchy, breathable fabrics. Prices €100 – 150 range.

www.sara-menonove.com

Vintage & Second-hand Clothes

A quick clarifying note: 'vintage' refers to items produced 20 or more years ago. Articles younger than 20 years are referred to as 'second-hand'.

In general, vintage clothes have a higher value not only because they are more antique, but due to the uniqueness of the pieces and the high quality of production that is often lacking in today's market. This is especially true of luxury brands whose prices tend to be higher than expected for goods that are not new.

Most vintage shops have a mix of goods: designer label pieces as well as no-name pieces. Just to give you an idea, second-hand no-name goods may start at €10, whereas vintage designer goods may start at €80.

This is an exhaustive list of all the vintage shops in Florence. For practical reasons I list the stores starting from the most central locations. The quaintest stores or the ones where I think you might find some great buys are indicated by an asterisk (*).

Most central

Street Doing – vintage couture *
where via dei Servi, 88r (near p. Santissima Annunziata)
store hours Tue – Sat 10:30 – 7:30, Mon - Sun. 2:30 – 7:30
phone 055 09 44 741

This is one the largest and most impressive vintage stores. The selection of clothes, shoes, bags, accessories is huge and of very high quality. You can also find plenty of designer labels: Florentine, Italian and foreign. There's also a small room dedicated to vintage lingerie. Items run the gamut from simple everyday wear to the most bizarre choices, all arranged in a very pleasant and easy to browse atmosphere.

www.streetdoingvintage.it

A.N.G.E.L.O. Vintage Clothing
where via dei Cimatori, 25r (just off via Calzaiuoli)
store hours Tue – Sat 10:30 – 7:30, Sun – Mon 3 – 7:30
phone 055 21 49 16

The main ANGELO store is in Ravenna and is a vintage emporium that is huge and even rents out its clothes and accessories for film and TV studios needing period garb. The Florentine version is much smaller and doesn't rent out its goods, but has a nice selection (also menswear) of unique pieces, elegant outfits, some designer labels and plenty of accessories.

www.angelo.it

Clochard (since **1970**) *
where via dei Conti, 16r (between p. Madonna and v. Cerretani)
store hours 10 – 1 & 3 – 7, Mon 3:30 – 7, Thu & Sat 10 – 7, Sun closed
phone 055 21 78 94

The oldest vintage shop in Florence, this is more second-hand store than vintage really. You can find older pieces but a lot of the items are relatively new too. This is also the most reasonably priced vintage store (by far) in town, and you can also find brand name stuff. Just across the street is 'Desii Vintage' (see below).

Melrose Vintage
where via Ginori, 18r (near p. San Lorenzo)
store hours 11 – 8   Sat 11:30 – 8:30   Sun 3 - 8
phone 055 26 700 30

A very showy vintage store (notice the fake rain at the shop entrance and the large motorcycle parked inside) that has more casual, sporty and American styles. Lots of jeans, cowboy boots and army garb.

www.melrosevintage.it

l'Chiodo (near p. Santa Croce)
where via dell'Anguillara, 39r (nearish p. Santa Croce)
store hours Mon 3:30 – 7:30   Tues - Sat 10:30 – 7:30
phone   055 28 56 52

l'Chiodo sells vintage clothes from the 50's to the 90's for men and women. Giulia and Brando, the owners, also customize clothes by applying studs, beads, rhinestones and other embellishings to sneakers, jeans, skirts, jackets, bags – whatever you bring in to them really. Here you can find brand name vintage as well as no-name articles and also bags, accessories, rings, bracelets, hats, belts, and more.

www.abbigliamentovintagefirenze.it

Fairly central

Vintage *
where piazzetta Calamandrei, 2 (near piazza Salvemini, off Borgo degli Albizi)
store hours 10:30 - 1:30 & 3 - 7:30 (closed Mon mornings & Sun)
phone 055 23 43 927

When you walk in this shop looks tiny, then you go downstairs and it's the basement where most of the clothes are kept. Some bags, shoes, belts and accessories and several racks of vintage and second-hand clothes. Some designer labels (I found a Max Mara skirt for €25) but most of the stuff is no-frills. Reasonable prices with some €10 racks.

A Ritroso *
where via Ghibellina 24r (nearish home of Michelangelo)
store hours Mon 4 – 7   Tue – Fri 10 – 1 & 4 - 7
phone 055 24 39 41

A lovely little vintage boutique with clothes and accessories dating between 1850 - 1980.   Everyday wear and evening dresses.   Collection of Florentine tailor-made suits and dresses from the 50's – 70's. Designer scarves from the 60's (Hermés, Pucci). Vintage hats from turn of the century.

Lady Jane B. *
where via dei Pilastri, 32b (near piazza Sant'Ambrogio)
store hours 3 – 8   (closed Tue and Sun)
phone 055 24 28 63

Very nicely set up shop, quaint and pleasant to browse in. Large rack for evening dresses and lots of accessories. Very affordable prices.

fb: LadyjaneBvintage

Belle Epoque
where Borgo Pinti, 24b (near p. Salvemini)
store hours 10:30 – 1 and 4 – 8 (Closed Mon mornings, Sat and Sun)

A very big store. Vintage clothes from the turn of the century, high-level custom tailored outfits and casual and sports wear from the 60's and 70's. Also second-hand clothes.

Also:
- **Epoca Vintage**, via dei Fossi, 6r (near p. Goldoni, along river) Mon – Sat 10 – 7:30, Sun 3:30 – 7:30

Slightly out-of-center

Milch Strasse *
where via Fra' Bartolomeo, 7r (near piazza della Libertà)
store hours Mon – Fri 10:30 – 7:15   Sat 10:30 – 1
phone 055 58 80 91

A shop for vintage, second-hand, and vintage designer clothes that has been open for 30 years. A very nice selection of top designer bags (I found a fabulous Gucci bag from the 70's in mint condition for €110). The ladies designer clothes are in very good condition (jackets, dresses and suits by Luisa Spagnoli, Pucci, Cavalli, Marina Rinaldi, Miu Miu, etc.). Also a huge selection of 'regular' clothes – casual and dressy – with items starting at €10. Large rack of ladies dresses for €30 each. Ask Rita, the owner, to show you the nicest stuff she's got (like lots of vintage stores, there's so much to look through you could easily miss those really special purchases).

By bus: no. 17 (direction 'Verga') to stop 'Fra' Bartolommeo 01 - Hotel San Gallo Palace'. If you get on in San Marco square in front of 'Pugi' bakery, you get off at the 2nd stop.

Walking: from piazza San Marco, at the right of the church, take via La Pira - which eventually becomes via Lamarmora - to the end, cross wide avenue, via fra' Bartolomeo is on other side.

Across the Arno river

Ceri Vintage
where via dei Serragli, 26r (just over ponte della Carraia)
store hours 10 - 12:30 & 3:30 – 7 (closed Mon morning & Sun)

A large cavernous space full of all sorts of unique stuff such as period uniforms, military items and one-of-a-kind pieces like Victorian corsets or women's hats with ostrich feathers. This is the vintage store with the largest selection of **menswear.**

Vintage by Celeste
where piazza San Felice, 1r (just past piazza Pitti)
store hours 10 – 1:30 and 3 – 7:30 (Mon only in pm, Sun closed)
phone 055 05 00 731

Vintage designer bags by top Italian labels. Suits, dresses, blouses, shirts, trousers, shoes and accessories (designer labels and not).

Also
- **Vintage Verabis**, via Maggio, 33r (over ponte S. Trinità) 11- 8 (closed Mon – Tue)
- **Custom Old Fashion***, via Romana, 142r (not far from Porta Romana), tel. 055 233 72 35, very retro shop with groovy atmosphere and lots of cool stuff.

Vintage Designer Label Clothes

The shops below deal exclusively in vintage and second-hand **designer and luxury goods**. Often the vintage pieces are in very good condition and you might find a Gucci or Prada bag or a Pucci dress for under €200.

DESII Vintage
where via dei Conti, 17r (just off via de' Cerretani)
store hours Mon - Wed 11:30 - 7:30, Thu - Sat 10:30 - 7:30
phone 055 23 02 817

A vintage store dedicated to clothes, bags and accessories of the most prestigious fashion houses (Pucci, Gucci, Ferragamo, Louis Vitton, Prada, etc). Items may be vintage (e.g. from the 70's or 80's) or from a few years ago. Worth a visit, even just to look at some of the eccentric pieces.

Elio Ferraro
where via del Parione, 47r
store hours 9:30 – 7:30 (closed Sun)
phone 055 29 04 25

After working for Ferragamo and Pucci, Elio Ferraro decided to use his knowledge and contacts to open a shop dedicated to vintage designer labels. Some rare pieces go back to early 1900's whereas the majority are from the 70's – 90's. Pucci, Gucci, Valentino, Chanel, YSL just to name a few.

www.elioferraro.com

Il Mercatino di Ninni
where via Cimabue, 24r (piazza Beccaria - via Gioberti area)
store hours 10 – 1 and 3:30 – 7 (closed Mon mornings and Sun)
phone 055 65 50 741

A smallish store jam-packed with second-hand designer clothes. If you have the patience to look through all the racks for some great buys it could really be worth it. Alternatively, you can ask the owner to show you some things, tell her the sort of outfit you're looking for and she'll start pulling out some great pieces (I found a magnificent black leather Max Mara skirt/jacket suit that looked brand new for only €200). Designer suits, coats, evening dresses, jackets.

By bus: the mini-buses 'C2' and 'C3' both go to piazza Beccaria (which is the last stop for both)

La Bottega dei Dolci Ricordi ('the boutique of sweet memories')
where via Squarcialupi, 5r (near piazza Puccini)
store hours 9:30 – 12 .30 & 3:30 – 7:30 (closed Mon morning & Sun)

This unique boutique specializes in second-hand and vintage designer handbags. You can find used bags, purses and wallets in good condition by Italian and foreign labels: Gucci, Prada, Dolce & Gabbana, Cavalli, Fendi, Alviero Martini, Chanel, Louis Vitton, Yves Saint Laurent, etc. The shop has new items every week so you never know what's going to be on offer. However, there are always at least 10 to 15 top label bags available. Items go for a fraction of their original cost (from €40 up) depending on the condition and year of the model.

Also: designer scarves

How to get there: short taxi ride from station (5 mins) or one of several buses: no. 17 (direction 'Boito' or 'Cascine') - get no. 17 at station near escalators at the pharmacy side of station - or any of buses no. 29 , 30, or 35 which all stop in via Alamanni on the tram side of the station. Bus stop is a block away from steps leading up to station entrance, walk in direction of the tram rails and via Alamanni is the street on the right when the road forks. Get off the bus at 'via Toselli' stop (there's a fenced-in parking lot right in front of the bus stop). From the bus stop walk back along via Toselli in the direction you came from to via Lulli (2 corners from the bus stop) and turn right — shop is 2 blocks down.

www.bottegadolciricordi.it

Seamstress & Tailor Workshops

'Sarta' means seamstress/tailor so a 'sartoria' is where clothes are made. These are shops where the clothes are all designed and sewn by the owners of the shop. You can find some wonderful work and unique items in these shops. Most sartoria have prices starting in the €60 - 100 range

Very central

Geraldine Tayar (since **2000**)
where sdrucciolo dei Pitti 6r (just off piazza Pitti)
store hours 9 – 7
phone 055 29 04 05

A tiny boutique with clothes for women. This shop carries very few pieces but they're all lovely, made of fine-quality fabrics styled into classic skirts, dresses and blouses. Since they don't produce in bulk they might not have your size, but if they do it's your lucky day. A very spartan but welcoming atmosphere.

Valditevere (since **1951**)
where via delle Terme, 15r (near p. Santa Trinità)
Store hours Mon 2 – 7 Tue – Sat 10 - 7
phone 055 28 27 07

This is a cozy boutique with a small selection of wonderful garments all created in the store with fabrics made of natural fibers such as linen, wool, cotton and silk. Perfect for the woman who likes to dress handsomely. More mature styles but also classic cuts that suit everyone.

www.valditevere.it

Giorgia (since **1990's**)
where via de' Ginori, 58r (parallel to via Cavour), also in via dei Servi, 77
store hours 10 – 2 and 3:30 – 7:30   Sun closed
phone 055 28 03 74

Giorgia is a long-standing shop making women's clothes in a very girlish free-spirited style (lots of floral patterns, bright colors and flouncy cuts).   Shop has a very large selection of hand-made accessories that are impressive (earrings, bags, hats, scarves, bracelets, brooches, and more).   The via Ginori shop is the original one, the via dei Servi store has the larger selection of accessories.

Across the Arno river

Quelle Tre (since **1989**) *
where via Santo Spirito 42r (near p. Santo Spirito)
store hours Tue – Sat 10:30 – 1:30 & 3 – 7, Sat opens at 11
phone 055 21 93 74

One of Florence's most popular 'sartoria', this shop has been written up in several magazines and books celebrating Tuscan artisans. Three sisters who come from a family of tailors have carried on the tradition making clothes in more contemporary creative styles. The clothing is a mix of traditional and modern cuts (probably more of the latter, with wide-leg pants, bat-wing tops, reversible shawls, fold-over blouses, etc.). A highly recommended store with a welcoming atmosphere and thoroughly artisan ambience.   Lovely pieces for children too.

www.quelletre.it

Giofrè (since **2000**)
where via Sant'Agostino, 30r (near piazza Santo Spirito)
store hours Mon – Fri 10 – 8, Sat & Sun opens 10:30
phone 055 23 99 141

This sartoria has a varied mix of styles: straight-forward white button-up shirts, traditional black blazers, as well as eccentric dresses in off-beat geometric patterns or blouses with one regular sleeve and the other short, this type of thing. You can find classic white, black and beige as well as bright color combinations. Giofrè is a good representation of Italian style: natural fabrics, high-quality workmanship and traditional ideas with (or without) a new twist. Also, great prices in the €50 - 80 range. Clothes for men & women.

www.giofrefashion.com

Le Zebre (the Zebras)
where via Romana, 88r (nearish Porta Romana)
store hours 10:30 – 8 (in August closed Sat-Sun, in winter closed Mon morning & Sunday)
phone 055 22 86 386

The clothes in this boutique are hand-painted and decorated by the owners (who also design and sew the garments). According to Francesca, the owner, their average customer is in the 30 - 40 age group, as the clothes tend to have a playful look and follow the latest trends. They have lovely and very feminine skirt and top sets and some blousy dresses in a sort of renewed 50's style. Overall a very varied mix of fun and unique stuff. Very reasonable prices.

www.lezebre.it

L'Abito che Vorrei ('the dress that I would like')
where via Romana, 62r (near via Romana entrance to Boboli gardens)
store hours Mon – Sat 11 – 7

Giuliana Becattini, the owner, makes clothes for women that are a mix of traditional, elegant, slim-lined tailored clothes and everyday wear. Even the casual clothes however have a certain class, and are conceived for the fashion-conscious woman looking for wardrobe with clean simple lines. Giuliana also makes a special attempt to create pieces that are easy-to-wear and practical. The boutique itself is lovely with some art-deco pieces and white furnishings.

www.labitochevorrei.it

Newer boutiques – less traditional (all centrally located)

Amo Romeo ('I love Romeo')
where via Verdi, 40r (nearish p. Santa Croce)
store hours 10:30 - 7   Mon 3 – 7   Sun closed
phone 055 24 10 11

A boutique with a fun personality (the shop is represented by a kooky frog, alias Romeo) where the young women who recently opened this shop make the clothing, bags and accessories. Garments are an assortment of modern cuts with a linear avant-garde style or baggy and loose fitting in a freer look. They only produce a few pieces of each garment so you really feel like you have bought something unique.

Pesci che volano ('Flying fish')
where borgo Pinti, 33r (street behind Pergola theater)
store hours Mon – Sat 10 – 1 & 3 - 7

This is a shop with its own identity, which prides itself on its originality. Most of the pieces are in wool (in summer there are some lighter materials such as linen or cotton) and their clothes for women are loose, wide-fitting and free-flowing (lots of Turkish style trousers with wide legs, low crotch, and narrow at the ankles). They also have hand-made knitwear (hats, bags, scarves, clothes). This boutique is great for comfortable (not form-fitting) but stylish clothes with an unusual flair.

The shop also has its own line of jewelry (with its fish symbol) made in bronze, ebony or silver that anyone who likes creative pieces will appreciate.

Very reasonable prices, between €30 – 80 for summer collection, jewelry €30 - 50.

Mrs Macis
where borgo Pinti, 38r (street behind Pergola theater)
store hours 10:30 – 1 and 4 – 7:30
phone 055 24 76 700

This boutique is like a burst of colors. The clothes here are definitely not the typical Italian look (they are more Spanish inspired, with lots of shades of red). Carla, the seamstress, also likes patchwork styles, retro patterns (polka-dots, stripes in all directions) and fun touches (eg pockets on a dress in the shape of hands). Admittedly, not everyone can get away with wearing this type of clothing, but if you are one of those who can, you'll love Mrs Macis.

Silk & Cashmere

There are plenty of silk scarves and cashmere knits around Florence that look good when you buy them but which start deteriorating after the first washing. If you're looking for something that will last longer but still with contained costs these shops might be for you.

Four rooms
where via Ventisette Aprile, 57r (near p. Indipendenza)
store hours Mon 3.30 – 7 Tue – Sat 10 .30 – 7
phone 055 46 18 31

A lovely boutique specializing in silk garments for women. The clothes are designed and made-in-Italy but many items have an ethnic flavor, Asian or African inspired. Also lovely stoles, shawls, cushion coverings and other articles made in glossy silk fabrics and bright strong colors. Inexpensive small items, such as wallets in silk, make nice gifts. **Prices:** reasonable

3 shops below are all in the same area:

In Seta (since **1987**)
where via della Vigna Nuova, 85r
store hours Mon 3:30 – 7:30   Tue – Sat 9:30 – 7:30
phone 055 21 07 31

Silk and silk-cashmere mix scarves. The 'In Seta' factory in Como produces for world-renowned designers (Fendi, Coveri, Pucci, Valentino, Cavalli, Ferré, Armani, Moschino, and others) as well as their own brands. If you want a quality scarf this shop has it all at very competitive prices. Shop assistants Fabiola and Silvia are very helpful. Also ties, stoles and Pashmina shawls in cashmere and a small clothing section.

G.B. Frugone (since **1885**)
where via delle Belle Donne, 35r
store hours Mon 3 – 7 Tue – Sat 10 – 7
phone 055 28 78 20

Knits in 100% cashmere for men and women. The shop has a large and varied selection of classic style sweaters, cardigans, stoles and shawls. Also items in silk/cashmere mix, linen and cotton. Competitive prices (eg men's pullovers start at €145) and store offers 50% off end-of-collection pieces all year.

Faliero Sarti
where via della Spada, 24r
store hours Mon 3 – 7:30 Tue – Sat 10 – 7:30 open last Sunday of the month 11 - 7
phone 055 23 96 538

The Tuscan designer Faliero Sarti is famous for his scarves and stoles. Cashmere, silk, alpaca and combinations of these, along with patterns and designs that are refined, subtle and highly contemporary make for his immediately recognizable look (truly gorgeous). The scarves are vast, creating plenty of delicate folds when wrapped. **Prices:** approx. €175 (but there's an outlet with lower prices, see 'Out-of-town Outlet Villages' chapter).

www.falierosarti.com

Out-of-Town Outlet Villages

Outlet villages are large shopping centers that sell brand name items that have been on the market for at least one year at reduced prices (30 to 70% off).

Outlets have been built to resemble quaint little towns in the countryside. The shopping centers are located in scenic areas and make for a very pleasant day out.

You will find everything you need: cafés, restaurants, bars, green areas for sitting and relaxing, free parking, play areas for children, services for people with reduced mobility, and staff who speak several languages.

1) The Mall
Via Europa, 8 – Leccio, Reggello
phone   055 86 57 775
www.themall.it

Open: everyday from 10 to 7
Closed: January 1, Easter Sunday, April 25 (liberation day), May 1 (labor day), December 25/26

For special opening hours see: *www.themall.it/en/visit*

For luxury brands, The Mall is number one as far as outlet centers go. There are only 25 stores, but they are all luxury brand shops which makes this outlet the most popular by far, with locals and tourists alike.

Some of the most popular brands are: Gucci, Pucci, Ferragamo, Armani and Fendi. For a complete list of labels see: *www.themall.it/en/brands/*

How to get to The Mall

By bus:
Coaches leave everyday from the 'Sita' bus depot right near the Santa Maria Novella station. The Sita station is in via Santa Caterina da Siena, 17 which is on the tram side of the station. Across from the tramway, on the corner is a large coffee shop called 'Bar Deanna'. The Sita depot is around the corner from this café.

Cost for a single ticket: €5

The trip takes just under an hour, and buses go from about 8:30 am – 6 pm.

By car:
From Florence take the highway 'A1' going in the direction of Rome and get off at the "Incisa-Reggello" exit. Stay on the road on the right going towards Pontassieve. Once you have passed Leccio, The Mall is on the left.

By train:
From the main train station, Santa Maria Novella, take a train to Rignano Sull'Arno. This stop is on the Florence – Arezzo line. From the Rignano sull'Arno station get a taxi to The Mall at taxi stand near station (about 5 minute ride, approx. €10).

2) Barberino Designer Outlet, Muggello
Via Meucci snc - 50031 Barberino del Mugello
phone 055 84 21 61

www.mcarthurglen.it/barberino/en

Opening hours:
Mon 2 - 8 (only from June to September and in December and January, closed on Mondays in other months)
Tue - Fri 10 – 8
Sat & Sun 10 – 9

The Barberino Outlet is has a very wide selection with over 100 stores.

However, it's probably most famous for having the two outlet shops of the celebrated Italian designers **'Prada'** and **'Dolce & Gabbana'**.

Full list of labels at www.mcarthurglen.it/barberino/en/brands.

How to get to the Barberino outlet:

Shuttle bus from Florence:
The bus stop is just outside the train station, Santa Maria Novella. The stop is in piazza della Stazione, at the end of via Nazionale, on the side of the large shoe store called 'Bata'. Cost for two-way ticket: €14 (buy ticket on bus)

Bus leaves twice a day at 10am and 2:30pm (trip takes 40 mins.). Bus leaves outlet to Florence at 1:30pm and 6:00pm

By car:
Take highway 'A1' from Florence going in the direction of Bologna. Get off at Barberino di Mugello exit. At the first roundabout take the second exit onto 'Viale del Lago' towards Barberino. Keep to the left to stay on 'Viale del Lago'. At the next roundabout take the second exit onto 'Via Antonio Meucci'. Keep to the right to stay on Via Meucci.

Outlet Stores

These are not shopping centers with several shops, but stores selling only their brand(s).

Prada:

The Space Outlet
52025 Levanella - on route SS69 Montevarchi, Arezzo
phone   055 91 96 528

Sells Prada and Miu Miu bags, clothes, footwear and accessories, sunglasses, and perfume as well as the legendary British shoe brand Church's and 'Car Shoe' shoes.

Prices are non-negotiable and no sales are carried out at Christmas season or during summer sales period.

Open: everyday 10:30 – 7:30 (Saturday 9:30 – 7:30)
Saturday is the busiest day so expect crowds and perhaps a long wait to get in.
Closed: January 1, Easter Sunday, Aug 15th, Dec 25th/26th
On December 24th and 31st store may have shorter opening times – call to be sure.

How to get to the Prada outlet:

By car:
From Florence take the A1 highway going south (direction Arezzo/Rome). Get off at the 'Val d'arno' exit. Go in the direction of 'Montevarchi' (state road 69) and pass through Arezzo, Montevarchi and Levanella (town where stockhouse is located). Once you have finished passing through the town of Levanella (at the end of the residential area on the right there is

a gas station), take the first left (there will be signs saying 'the Space Outlet' Prada).

By train:
Take a train from the main Florence station, Santa Maria Novella, to Montevarchi. At the Montevarchi station get a taxi to Levanella, the Space outlet (just under 3 miles).

Outlet stores close to downtown Florence:

These outlet stores, while being a bit outside Florence, can all be reached with the Florence city buses (Ataf lines).

Nannini
Via Faentina, 77
phone 055 46 39 452
www.nannini.it

Nannini is a Florentine company that made its name producing ladies handbags in suede and leather. The Nannini style is chic and cosmopolitan with quality leather and fine finishings, a refined and elegant look. Now Nannini have branched out into shoes, boots and accessories (wallets, belts, key chains, etc.).

Open: 10 – 7 (closed on Sundays)
During the Christmas season and summer open til later and on Sundays too, so phone to check.

How to get there by bus:
- Bus no. 1A direction 'Salviati' – get off at the 'Caracciolo' stop, go back a few feet to the corner and turn right into via del Ponte alle Riffe, walk straight then turn right into via Faentina.
- Bus no. 1B direction 'Boccaccio' - get off at the 'Madonna della Querce' stop, just keep walking in same direction (street

becomes via del Ponte alle Riffe after you cross the bridge) then turn right into via Faentina.

L'Accessorio di Faliero Sarti
Via Vittorio Alfieri, 88 - Campi Bisenzio
phone   055 89 66 250
www.falierosarti.com

Open: Mon – Fri 9 – 1 and 2 – 6

A luxury Florentine brand for cashmere and cashmere-silk mix scarves with an ultra-modern appeal.
If you want to check out the 'Sarti' style before going to the outlet store, the shop is in via della Spada 24r.

Getting there by bus:
In via Alamanni take bus number 30B (near the tram side of the station, walk in the same direction as the tram rails going away from the station, the road forks and the rails go left, via Alamanni is the street on the right). Get off at the stop 'Tosca Fiesoli 04' (approx. a 30 minute ride, then a 15 minute walk). Walk ahead to the roundabout and take the first street on the right, via Barberinese, then take the first left, via Castronella, then take the second right, via Vittoria Alfieri and stay on this road till you get to no. 88.

Designer Label Stores

Via Tornabuoni and its neighboring streets have the greatest concentration of luxury brands and designer labels in Florence. This is the place to go for the biggest names and the best quality goods. The selection of shop names below aims to be more than just a list of addresses by giving the reader added information about the origins of the label and any additional information that might be helpful.

Allegri (Italy, Milan/Florence, **1960**)
Italian sportswear, coats, raincoats, trench coats, modernized Montgomery
where via Tornabuoni, 72r
store hours Mon 3 – 7 Tue – Sat 10 – 7
phone 055 23 81 004
www.allegri.it

Anne Fontaine (France, Paris, **1993**)
Fashion designer most known for giving innovative touches to the classic white shirt for women
where via Tornabuoni, 71r
store hours 10 – 7
phone 055 26 70 477
www.annefontaine.com

Armani (Italy, Milan, **1975**)
The king of casual elegance, unmistakable class and simplicity
where via Tornabuoni, 48r
store hours 10 – 7
phone 055 21 90 41
www.armani.com

Bottega Veneta (Italy, Vicenza, **1967**)
Luxury shoes, clothes, jewelry, bags and accessories
where via degli Strozzi, 6
store hours 10 – 7   Sun 2 – 7
phone 055 28 47 35
www.bottegaveneta.com

Bulgari (Italy, Rome, **1884**)
A luxury brand for fine jewels and accessories
where via Tornabuoni, 56r
store hours Mon – Sat 10 – 7
phone 055 23 96 789
www.bulgari.com

Burberry (United Kingdom, **1856**)
World renowned luxury brand for trench coats and outdoor
apparel yet with approachable prices
where via Tornabuoni, 31r
store hours 10:30 – 7:30
phone 055 29 38 11
www.burberry.com

Cartier (France, Paris, **1847**)
Luxury jewelers and watch makers
where via degli Strozzi, 36r
store hours 10 – 1:30 and 3 – 7   closed Sun mornings
phone 055 29 23 47
www.cartier.com

Casadei (Italy, Forli, **1958**)
Extremely feminine shoes distinguished by their strikingly high
heels, platforms and wedges
where via Tornabuoni, 33r
store hours Mon 3 – 7   Tue - Sat 10 – 1 and 2 - 7
phone 055 28 72 40
www.casadei.com

Céline (France, Paris, **1945**)
French luxury ready-to-wear fashion, bags and accessories
where via Tornabuoni, 26r
store hours Mon - Sat 10 – 7
phone 055 26 45 521
www.celine.com

Chanel (France, Paris, **1909**)
Parisian designer known for its sleek-lined looks and, of course,
its perfume Chanel no. 5.
where piazza della Signoria, 10
store hours Mon - Sat 10 – 7
phone 055 29 23 95
www.chanel.com

Damiani (Italy, Valenza, **1924**)
Three generations of Italian goldsmiths making luxury jewelry
and watches
where via Tornabuoni, 30r
hours Mon 3 – 7   Tue - Sat 10 – 1:30 and 3 - 7
phone 055 29 02 08
www.damiani.com

Desmo (Italy, Florence, **1976**)
Classic leather bags hand-crafted in Florence by local artisans –
see their signature 'Sara' purse
where via Tornabuoni, 7r
store hours Mon – Sat 10 – 7 (also last Sunday of the month)
phone 055 26 70 509
www.desmo.it

Dior (France, Paris, **1946**)
High fashion and luxury ready-to-wear items
where via Tornabuoni, 57r
store hours Mon – Sat 10 – 7
phone 055 26 69 101
www.dior.com

Dolce & Gabbana (Italy, Milan, **1985**)
Enormously popular Italian brand known for its innovative looks
and unpredictable creations
where via degli Strozzi, 12
store hours Mon – Sat 10 – 7
phone 055 28 10 03
www.dolcegabbana.com

Ermanno Scervino (Italy, Firenze, **1997**)
Florentine luxury brand for knitwear and ready-to-wear attire
where piazza degli Antinori, 10r
store hours 10 – 7:30   Sun 3 – 7
phone 055 26 08 714
www.ermannoscervino.it

Ermenegildo Zegna (Italy, Trivero, **1910**)
One of the top Italian fashion houses specializing in men's clothing
where via Tornabuoni, 3r
store hours Mon – Sat 10 – 7, Sun 2 – 7
phone 055 26 42 54
www.zegna.com

Fani Gioielli (Italy, Florence, **1950s**)
A family run Florentine silver shop has evolved into a luxury store for jewelry and Rolex watches
where via Tornabuoni, 101r
store hours Mon 3 – 7 Tues – Sat 10 – 7
phone 055 21 20 75
www.fanishops.it

Fendi (Italy, Rome, **1925**)
Luxury brand famous for its handbags with the double 'f' logo
where via degli Strozzi, 21r
store hours 10 – 7:30   Sun opens at 11
phone 055 21 23 05
www.fendi.com

Ferragamo (Italy, Florence, **1928**)
Luxury Florentine shoes - visit the Ferragamo shoe museum in same building
where via Tornabuoni, 4 - 14r
store hours Mon – Sat 10 – 7:30, Sun 2 - 7
phone 055 29 21 23
www.ferragamo.com

Furla (Italy, Bologna, **1927**)
Italian luxury brand for leather bags
where via Calzaiuoli, 49r
store hours 10 – 7
phone 055 23 82 883
www.furla.com

Gherardini (Italy, Florence, **1885**)
Designer bags for women with the 'G' logo known for their
trademark 'Softy' material
where via della Vigna Nuova, 57r
store hours Tues – Sat 10 – 7 Mon opens at 3:30
phone 055 21 56 78
www.gherardini.it

Guess (U.S.A., Los Angeles, **1981**)
One of the first brands to produce designer jeans
where via Vecchietti, 17r
store hours 10 – 7:30, Sun opens at 11
phone 055 21 11 85
www.guess.com

Gucci (Italy, Florence, **1921**)
Flagship store of the Florentine luxury brand – most popular
Italian designer worldwide
where via Tornabuoni, 73 - 81r
store hours 10 – 7
phone 055 26 40 11
www.gucci.com

Hermès (France, Paris, **1837**)
Initially a maker of harnesses and bridles for horses, now known
for bags, scarves and luxury goods
where piazza degli Antinori, 6r
store hours Mon – Sat 10 – 7
phone 055 23 81 004
www.hermes.com

Hogan (Italy, Le Marche, **1980**)
an Italian twist on sneakers: super comfy yet stylish walking
shoes
where via Tornabuoni, 97r (located in a historical landmark
building once an English pharmacy)
store hours Mon – Sat 10 – 7:30   Sun 2 - 7
phone 055 27 41 013
www.hogan.com

Les Copains (Italy, Bologna, **1950**)
Italian high fashion clothing, most notably cashmere knitwear
where piazza degli Antinori, 2-3r
store hours Mon 3 – 7, Tue – Sat 10 – 7
phone 055 29 29 85
www.lescopains.it

Locman (Italy, Elba Island, **1986**)
Prestigious watches combine state-of-the-art technology and
Italian craftsmanship
where via Tornabuoni, 76r
store hours Mon – Sat 10 – 7
phone 055 21 16 05
www.locman.it

Loretta Caponi (Italy, Florence, **1986**)
Exquisite hand sewn lace and embroidered linens and lingerie
where piazza degli Antinori, 4r
phone 055 21 10 74
store hours Mon – Sat 10 – 7
www.lorettacaponi.it

Loro Piana (Italy, Quarona, **1924**)
The epitome of Italian elegance and quality in clothes,
especially known for cashmere knits
where via della Vigna Nuova, 37r
phone 055 23 98 688
store hours Mon – Sat 10 – 7
www.loropiana.com

Liu Jo (Italy, Modena, **1995**)
A relatively young yet very popular Italian fashion brand for
clothes and bags
where via Calimala, 12r
phone 055 21 61 64
store hours Mon – Sat 10 - 7:30   Sun 11 – 7:30
www.liujo.com

Louis Vuitton (France, Paris, **1854**)
French brand known for its ever-popular brown canvas bags
with the LV logo
where piazza degli Strozzi, 1
phone 055 26 69 81
store hours Mon – Sat 10 - 7:30   Sun 11 – 7:30
www.louisvuitton.com

Luisa Spagnoli (Italy, Perugia, **1928**)
One of Italy's most appreciated brands for classic ladies clothes
Trivia: the founder, Luisa Spagnoli, also invented the 'bacio perugina' chocolate bon bon
where via dei Calzaiuoli, 32r (also in via degli Strozzi)
phone 055 21 38 57
store hours Mon – Sat 9:30 – 7:30, Sun 11 - 7
www.luisaspagnoli.com

Max Mara (Italy, Reggio Emilia, **1951**)
Extremely popular brand - a big name yet approachable prices
where via Tornabuoni, 70r
phone 055 21 41 33
store hours Mon – Sat 10 – 7:30   Sun 11 - 7
www.maxmara.com

Missoni (Italy, Lombardy, **1953**)
Designer knits created with the company's famous zigzag pattern in a kaleidoscope of colors
where via Porta Rossa, 77r
phone 055 21 57 74
store hours 10 – 7:30
www.missoni.com

Moschino (Italy, near Rimini, **1983**)
The unconventional and fun-spirited Moschino brand can be bought in the shops:
  Carpe Diem (extremely large selection of clothes and accessories by Moschino)
  where via Ricasoli, 52r
  phone 055 29 22 81
  store hours Tue – Sat 10 – 2 & 3 - 7

'Spazio A'
where via Porta Rossa, 107r
phone 055 21 29 95
store hours Mon – Sat 10 – 7

www.moschino.com

Patrizia Pepe (Italy, Florence, **1993**)
Relatively new yet very popular Florentine label for women,
approachable prices
where via degli Strozzi, 13r
phone 055 23 02 518
store hours 10 – 7:30
www.patriziapepe.com

Pomellato (Italy, Milan, **1967**)
Jewelry designed and made in Italy in all types of metals
where via Tornabuoni, 89r
phone 055 28 85 30
store hours Mon – Sat 10 – 7
www.pomellato.com

Prada (Italy, Milan, **1913**)
Who hasn't heard of the coveted Prada bags with their world
famous triangle logo?
where via Tornabuoni, 53-67r
phone 055 26 74 71
store hours 10 – 7
www.prada.com

Pucci (Italy, Florence, **1947**)
Florentine designer whose geometric prints and bright color
schemes are instantly recognizable
Trivia: Marilyn Monroe was buried in a green Pucci dress
where via Tornabuoni, 22r
phone 055 26 58 082
store hours Mon - Sat 10 – 7 (also last Sunday of the month)
www.pucci.com

Raspini (Italy, Florence, **1946**)
Shoes are Raspini's claim to fame – elegant classic styles for
men and women
where via Roma, 25r
phone 055 21 30 77
store hours 10:30 – 7:30

Note: at **Raspini Vintage** (in spite of name, this is not a store
that sells vintage clothes) you can find lower prices on large
selection of designer labels.
where via Calimaruzza, 17r
phone 055 21 39 01
store hours Mon – Sat 10:30 – 7:30 (this is the official time,
although I often find it closed!)
www.raspini.com

Roberto Cavalli (Italy, Florence, **1970**)
Renowned Florentine designer known for his animal prints and
signature sand-blasted jeans
where via Tornabuoni, 83r
phone 055 23 96 226
store hours Mon – Sat 10 – 7 (also last Sunday of month)
www.robertocavalli.com

Seguso Archimede (Italy, Venice, **1946**)
Murano artistic glass furnishings
where via dei Rondinelli, 3r
store hours Mon 11 – 7   Tue – Sat 10 – 7
phone 055 28 34 67
www.aseguso.com

Sergio Rossi (Italy, Romagna, **1950**)
Luxury Italian shoes styled by designers and made by artisans
where via Tornabuoni, 37r
store hours 10 – 7
phone 055 28 46 31
www.sergiorossi.com

Swarovski (Austria, **1895**)
Crystals and jewelry
where via dei Rondinelli, 8r
store hours Tue – Sat 10 – 1:30 and 2:30 – 7:30
phone 055 21 52 61
www.swarovski.com

The Bridge (Florence, Italy, **1969**)
Named after the beloved 'Ponte Vecchio', maker of leather
bags in trademark toasty brown color
where via Valchereccia, 17r
store hours Mon – Sat 10 – 7
phone 055 21 60 88
www.thebridge.it

Tiffany & Co. (the U.S.A, **1837**)
New York jewelry company famous worldwide for diamonds
where via Tornabuoni, 25r
store hours Mon – Sat 10 – 7
phone 055 21 55 06
www.tiffany.com

Tod's (Italy, Le Marche, **1920s**)
The classic 'informally elegant' Italian shoe
where via Tornabuoni, 60r
store hours Mon – Sat 10 – 7:30   Sun 2 - 7
phone 055 21 94 23
www.tods.com

Tommy Hilfiger (U.S.A., New York, **1984**)
American style casual wear
where piazza degli Antinori, 3D
store hours 10 – 7
phone 055 27 41 041
www.tommyhilfiger.com

Department Stores

There are three main department stores in Florence:

La Rinascente
where Piazza delle Repubblica
store hours 9 – 9   Sun 10:30 – 8
phone 055 21 91 13

This is the department store with the highest quality goods and the most variety.   Rinascente has made its long-standing reputation by selling only top quality items and designer labels (see site for list of brands).

There are special sections for younger styles, classic looks, and plus size clothes (on the 3rd floor).   There's a large cosmetics area on the ground floor with the leading brands of make-up and luxury beauty products, and a top floor with a wonderful selection of items for the house.

Take advantage of the special discount for foreign visitors: go to *www.rinascente.it* and click on 'international visitors' on the home page. You will get a 10% coupon that you can download to use in the store (you must show your passport with the coupon).

Coin
where via dei Calzaiuoli, 56r (near p. Repubblica)
store hours 10 – 8   Sun 10:30 – 8
phone 055 28 05 31

Coin is the middle road between Rinascente and Oviesse (below).   The store has almost as much selection as the

Rinascente and also carries many famous brands and plenty of quality items.

Its prices are a bit lower than the Rinascente and you can also find fashionable clothes that might have no famous designer name but which look just as good and go for a more reasonable cost. They have a larger menswear section and the house ware department is also very extensive. Coin also carries a specific brand, Anisette, which produces plus size clothing.

www.coin.it

Oviesse
where via Panzani, 31 (corner of via del Giglio, station area)

store hours 9 – 7:30
phone 055 23 98 963

This is a basic and unpretentious department store.

Oviesse produces its own clothes under the 'Oviesse' brand so you won't find famous designer names in the store. They offer down-to-earth fashions, good for finding simple classic pieces.

The prices are quite low. At *www.oviesse.it* you can check out the men's, women's and children's collections. They have an especially large section of clothes for babies, toddlers and young children. For teenage girls, they have their own brand – 'Baby Angel' – created by the designer Fiorucci which sells trendy young clothes.

The store also has a section for plus-size clothes.

Chain Stores

Florence has several chain stores where you can find great value as well as stylish clothes and other goods. While they might not have the individuality of a unique boutique, competitive prices make these stores a valid shopping choice. Goods are Italian design but often production is carried out overseas – check label.

Lingerie, sleepwear, tights, accessories

1) Goldenpoint
via Panzani 33r, via dei Calzaiuoli 51, via Cerretani 40
www.goldenpointonline.com

2) Yamamay
Piazza Unità d'Italia 20r, via dei Calzaiuoli 76r
www.yamamay.com

3) Intimissimi
via dei Calzaiuoli 99r
www.intimissimi.com

4) Tezenis
via dei Calzaiuoli 78r
www.tezenis.com

5) Calzedonia (only socks and tights – huge selection)
Via Panzani 58, Via dei Calzaiuoli 68r
www.calzedonia.it

Clothes

1) Sisley
via Cerretani 57, via Roma 11r
www.sisley.com

2) Benetton
via Piazza Stazione 16R, borgo San Lorenzo 17r
www.benetton.com

3) Camicissima (only shirts and knitwear)
via Panzani 53r, via dei Calzaiuoli 94r
www.camicissima.com

4) Nara Camice (only shirts)
Via Porta Rossa 25r
www.naracamicie.com

Handbags

1) Mandarina Duck
one of Italy's most loved labels for casual bags
via Cerrettani 64, via Por Santa Maria 23
www.mandarinaduck.com

2) Coccinelle
one of Italy's most loved labels for leather bags
via Calzaiuoli 28r
www.coccinelle.com

Footwear

1) Geox
magnificent shoes made with a special patent which allows feet
to breathe – comfort and great style.
Via Panzani 4, via Calimala 11
www.geox.com

2) Bata
classic Italian leather shoes at reasonable prices
corner of Largo Alinari and Piazza della Stazione
www.bata.it

Hats

Florence used to have a straw market, and making hats out of straw is another craft that the city was known for. Nowadays Florentine straw hats are harder to find (imported hats produced overseas abound however). There are however a few local hat-makers who still carry on this tradition and who produce hats in other materials as well.

Grevi (since **1875**)
where via della Spada, 11r
store hours 10 – 2 & 3 – 8, Sun closed
phone 055 26 41 39

The Grevi family have been making hats since 1875. Straw hats are their forté, both in simple traditional styles or a playful contemporary look. There's a special line for children's hats that are adorable.

Prices: start at €40

www.grevi.com

Antonio Gatto
where Piazza Pitti, 5
store hours Tue – Sat 10 – 1 and 4 – 7:30
phone 055 26 54 271

The only artisan hat maker in Florence whose shop is also his workshop. You can find straw hats for every day summer wear (he has a straw hat for travelling which can be flattened out in a suitcase without being ruined) to more extravagant and sophisticated styles. Antonio makes hats also for the theater and to be sold in the most exclusive stores in New York and Tokyo, yet has a very unassuming air and greets people warmly in his peaceful boutique.

Prices: start at approx. €100

www.antoniogatto.com

Shoes

There are almost as many shoe shops in Florence as there are leather bag stores. Really, it can get overwhelming.

Here's one tip: when you see stores selling cheap shoes (€20 range), look at the sole to see what's written. Does it say 'made in Italy'? If Italian shoes are what you want, don't assume that just buying from a store in Florence means that they are Italian made.

Here's a list of some of the most popular shoe shops where locals go. Pricewise, these stores sell shoes that range from €60 – 150. Men's shoes may go a bit higher whereas summer shoes and sandals should be significantly lower.

Classic looks

See also: subheading 'footwear' in the **'Artisan Leather Workshops'** chapter

Mazzuoli
where via Panzani, 20r (midway between station and Duomo)
store hours 9 - 7:30 Sun opens at 12:30
phone 055 28 49 54

This store is one of the old-faithfuls of Florence. It's been here forever probably because it has lots of selection, good quality, reasonable prices, is in a convenient location, and the staff aren't pushy. The shoes are aligned by size and you can handle them and try on as you like.

Enrico & Annalisa Materassi
where piazza San Lorenzo, 28r
store hours Mon – Sat 10:30 – 6:30 (Sat may close earlier)
phone 055 21 06 92

This shop has no sign and no visible street address written on the wall so I'll describe where it is: coming from piazza San Giovanni, you walk down borgo San Lorenzo, and it's the first shop on the right when you get to the square. You go down the (steep) steps and the store is in the basement (shoes are displayed outside though). Most of the shoes here are in the hallmark tanned rich leather that we associate with Italian quality. Casual, sporty, everyday shoes.

Renato Desii
where borgo San Lorenzo, 18r (on the right heading towards 'Enrico & Annalisa Materassi')
store hours 9:30 – 1:30 & 3:30 - 8
phone 055 28 43 71

This shop has been here for over 40 years. Desii tends to sell more conservative shoes in traditional styles (don't get confused with another shop called DESII on the same street which sells highly unusual shoes). Good for shoes to go with a business suit or ladies pumps.

Prices start at approx. €120.

NeroGiardini
where via Por Santa Maria, 64r (also in v. del Corso, 60r)
store hours 10 – 7:30   Sun 11- 7
phone 055 27 40 549

This Italian company has become an international firm exported all over the world but all material selection and manufacturing are carried out in Italy. These are easily the most popular (non-luxury) brand name shoes among Italians. Their leather boots (€150 range) and canvas/leather walking shoes (€90 range) are big sellers. Modern styles, elegant yet casual.

www.nerogiardini.it

Otisopse
where via Porta Rossa, 13r (and 3 other locations, see below)
store hours 10 – 1 and 2 – 7:30
phone 055 23 96 717

This shop only sells shoes produced on their own label in the family factory in Naples. The styles are classic and fairly conservative (ladies pumps with low heel, men's flat loafers).

Prices are low compared to other made-in-Italy brands (classic men's shoe for under €100).

Other stores:
Piazza Sauro 7r (across the street from this store is the **Otisopse outlet**: prices start at €10), Via Guicciardini 2r, Via dei Neri 58r

www.otisopse.it

Flashier, trendier, more contemporary shoes

See also: '**Mondo Albion**' in 'Special Mention' chapter and '**Sergio Rossi**' in 'Designer Label Stores' chapter

Onakò

where via Cerretani, 50r (also in via Calzaiuoli, 41r)
store hours 10 – 7:30, Sun opens at 11
phone 055 21 15 81

This is a relatively new shop which offers something different from the traditional shoe. Onakò sells unconventional looks (super high platform cork heels, patent leather embellished with colored stones, flats with lots of tie-up laces, boots with lots of zippers and laces, etc.) The name may not sound Italian, but all items are made-in-Italy.

Reasonable prices considering the trendy style.

www.onako.it

Cesare Paciotti

Where via della Vigna Nuova, 14r
Store hours Mon 3 – 7:30, Tue - Sat 9:30 – 1:30 & 3 – 7:30
Phone 055 21 54 71

Italian luxury brand of shoes most famous for its '4US' line of sporty shoes for men and women which brandishes the Paciotti logo: a sword. Comfortable to wear and super-cool to look at, these walking shoes are worn by people from 15 to 70 years old, with faded jeans or with Armani suits. One of my favorite Italian products.

Not cheap but worth the price as they last forever (close to €200).

www.cesare-paciotti.com

Calvani
where via degli Speziali, 7r (near p. Repubblica)
store hours 10 – 7:30, Sun 2:30 – 7:30
phone 055 26 54 043

If you want something **unconventional**, go here. This shop carries some brands that are not Italian. The non-Italian made shoes happen to be however of the utmost style and quality. Lots of the shoes here are what I would call 'chunky', clogs with thick wood platforms and brass stud finishings, boots with wide heels, etc. Then there are some styles that only slightly eccentric. There's also a big choice of original sneakers. The store is beautiful too with high ceilings and stony décor. High-end prices.

www.calvanifirenze.it

Two very popular shoe stores

The underground gallery located beneath the S.M.N. train station has two of Florence's most popular shoe stores for the latest trendy styles. These shops carry mixed brands with plenty of Italian shoes but also many imported labels.

Avantgarde
where near the waterfall fountain, the new part of the gallery, at no. 14
store hours Mon 10:30 - 7:30, Tue - Sat 9:30 - 7:30, Sun 3:30 - 7:30
phone   055 29 12 41

The variety of footwear that Avantgarde carries is uncommon. The shoes run the gamut from a modern twist on classic styles, to very trendy and bizarre Italian and international styles and

brands. The shop also has a section dedicated to walking shoes.
Price range from €100 up.

www.avantgardecalzature.it

R.M. 4
where in the older part of the gallery, near the men's and
ladies' toilets
store hours 9:30 – 7:30, Sun opens at 3:30
phone 055 23 98 521

A shoe store with a good selection of sporty or casual footwear
at reasonable prices but also a large choice of much more
unconventional shoes. If you like very high platform heels with
irregular forms, eccentric looks or just more original stuff you'll
want to check this shop out. Often has great bargains.   A long-
standing shop in Florence, tending towards a young look. Prices
between €50 – 130.

Accessories

Dettagli
where Borgo degli Albizi, 40r (this street is a continuation of v. del Corso)
store hours 10 – 7:30, Mon opens at 3:30, Sun opens at 1:30
phone 055 23 40 333

A very popular and long-standing store patronized by locals and tourists alike. Dettagli (which means 'details') has all sorts of lovely stuff to jazz up your look such as costume jewelry, purses, wallets and small evening bags, hair accessories, pins, brooches, scarves and lots more. The owners of the store make a lot of the articles themselves and the rest are made by artisans in the area. This is also a very fun store for just looking or for gift ideas.

Emanuela Biffoli
where via Rondinelli, 23r (near p. Antinori)
store hours Mon – Sat 10:30 – 7:30
phone 055 28 84 93

Emanuela Biffoli's main claim to fame is make-up brushes. But this is also a perfect shop for cute gift ideas (mostly for women) like compact mirrors in a rhinestone or snakeskin case, hand-made make up purses, imported exotic creams and body oils, soap and body lotion sets, and also accessories like scarves, hats, and original purses – all at low prices. Check out their web site to see the wide range of items you can find here. Prices on small items from 10€ to 25€.

www.biffoli.com

Déco
where via Donizetti, 24B (piazza Puccini)
store hours Tue – Sat 9:30 – 1 .30 and 3:30 – 7:30 (Mon open only in afternoon)
phone (cell) 328 359 66 33

This shop is **off the beaten path** so it might be a good idea to check out the web site before going to see if it's your cup of tea. Cristina is a local artist who hand-paints all the lovely items in her shop: hats, bags, purses, shoes, and home goods such as linens, lamp shades or wall decorations. She also makes accessories like brooches, belts and bracelets, all in her distinctive style (plenty of images on site). All items are made of natural materials, mostly straw in summer and wool in winter.

By taxi it should take no more than 5-10 minutes from the station or a 10 minute **bus ride**. Take bus no. 17 direction 'Cascine' or 'Boito' (from the station the bus stop is on the pharmacy side right near the escalators), or buses 29, 30 or 35 (taken from the side of station where tram is, in via Alamanni, about a block away from the station entrance). Get off in Piazza Puccini. Cross over to other side of the square, shop is near 'Cassa di Risparmio di Firenze' bank.

Prices: min €20 – max €70

http://decodicristinaturci.oneminutesite.it/

Other Fun Stuff

Books and CDs

These are specialty stores which might interest visitors to Florence.

Paperback Exchange – anglo-american bookshop (since **1979**)
where via delle Oche, 4r (first left in via dei Calzaiuoli coming from Duomo)
store hours Mon – Fri 9 – 7:30   Sat 10:30 – 7:30
phone 055 29 34 60

A very convenient store for English language books (also low priced second-hand books) and information about local events in English. The shop has a particularly good selection of titles dedicated to Florence, Tuscany and Italian art and culture. You can also pick up a free copy of the local English paper (the 'Florentine') at the shop which fills you in on local news and also provides tons of information about 'what's on' in Florence, museums, etc. all in English.

www.papex.it

B & M – books and fine art (since **1961**)
where Borgo Ognissanti, 4r (just off piazza Goldoni)
store hours Tue – Sat 10:30 – 7
phone 055 29 45 75

B & M opened in 1961 and is the oldest English language book shop in Florence. If you go to the website and click on the 'about us' link, you can see some dramatic photos of how the 1966 flood of Florence effected the shop (the shop location was on the same spot as it is today, just off the Arno river, so it was greatly affected by this historic event). This bookstore too has a large selection of books dedicated to Florence and Italy in general, especially Italian cooking. It also has a €5 euro bargain shelf with lots of used paperbacks.

www.bmbookshop.com

Fenice
where via Santa Reparata, 8b
hours Mon – Fri 9 – 1:30 & 3:30 – 7:30, Sat 9 – 1
phone 055 39 28 713

Named after Venice's famed opera house, this record store is a must for music lovers. Records, cds, and dvds of operas and classical music as well as books about the lives of famous composers, musicians and opera singers.

www.dischifenice.it

Souvenirs

Michelangelo Souvenirs (since **1993**)
where via Ricasoli, 75r (near piazza San Marco)
store hours 10 – 7   closed Mondays   Sun 10 - 2
phone 055 28 82 59

A souvenir shop dedicated exclusively to **made-in-Italy**. The shop carries some of the loveliest Florentine craftwork such as etchings, alabaster statuettes, hand-painted wood trays lined with gold foil, silk-screen prints on linen, hand-decorated bronze miniatures and more.   This is a quality souvenir shop (a rarity these days) operated by Florentines who have an earnest appreciation of the artwork and the historic city that the objects they sell represent. Prices are reasonable too.

www.michelangelosouvenirs.com

Vexus
where via della Scala, 15r (nearish Station)
store hours   Mon to Sat 9 – 1 and 3:30 - 7:30
phone   055 23 96 543

Guido Vezzosi, the shop owner, has been selling his wares in Florence for over 50 years; in fact, the shop has a bit of an old-fashioned feel.   However, it also has some of the very best prices for classic Florence souvenirs. Go here if you want to take home lots of trinkets for friends and family, you'll save a lot of money (eg postcards 25 cents, pocket calendars €1, book marks €1, etc.).

Gadgets

Controluce
where via della Vigna Nuova, 89r (near p. Goldoni)
store hours Tue – Sat 9:30 – 1:30 and 3 – 7:30   Monday open only in afternoon
phone 055 23 98 871

A very popular and memorable shop full of ingenious little gadgets for everyday use (folding ashtrays, light-up pocket make-up mirrors, computer paraphernalia, etc). The design and style of the gadgets are humorous, colorful and modern. Also lighting fixtures. Worth a visit and great for gift ideas. Prices surprisingly low.

www.controlucefirenze.it

Arti & Mestieri
where Borgo degli Albizi, 67r
store hours Tue – Sat   9:30 – 1:30 and 3 – 7:30   Monday open only in afternoon
phone 055 23 98 871

The shop owners (designer and architect) personally design all the items in the store. Very original and modern ideas for the home or any interior space (key hooks, book ends, photo frames, etc.). The shop has an especially large and impressive selection of wall and mantel clocks. Prices medium to high range.

www.artiemestieri.it

Street Markets

San Lorenzo Market
where streets around Piazza San Lorenzo
when: Mon – Sat 9 – 7 (also open on Sundays but with fewer stalls) in winter closed on Mondays

Florence's most well-known and most central market. Clothing, leather goods, souvenirs, scarves, shoes, stationery stands, ceramics and more. San Lorenzo is very popular with tourists but is also frequented by locals. Inside the 18th century building - which has its main entrance in Piazza del Mercato Centrale - there is a very popular food market where Florentines who live centrally do their shopping (closes at 2 pm). Here you can find some wonderful food stands that offer typical local foods at good prices.

Cascine Market
where at the Cascine park (the last stop of **bus no. 17** direction 'Cascine' drops you at the market)
when: every Tuesday 9 – 2 (open also on the four Sundays prior to Easter Sunday)

This is the market that is most popular with locals. Goods at the Cascine market are not aimed at tourists (ie no souvenir stalls). That makes it a good choice if you want an authentic market experience. Market sells clothing, shoes, house ware, linens, undergarments and sleepwear, cds and more. There are also lots of stands with foodstuff, cheeses, breads, cold cuts, fruits and vegetables.

'Porcellino' Market (aka 'Mercato Nuovo', the New Market)
where   via Porta Rossa meets via Calimala (heading towards Ponte Vecchio)
when: everyday 9 – 7

The Porcellino market is most famous for its bronze fountain of a wild boar that dates back to the 1640's. Legend goes that if you make a wish and rub the animal's nose while putting a coin in its mouth your wish will come true. This market is held under a loggia that goes back to the 1500's when it was built for the local silk and straw merchants.   Today it sells very similar items to the San Lorenzo market (but is much smaller) and is more frequented by tourists than locals.

San Ambrogio Market
where   piazza Sant'Ambrogio and Piazza Ghiberti
when: Mon – Sat 9 – 2

This is a true neighborhood market frequented mostly by people living in the area. Similarly to the Cascine market, along with clothes and shoes there are plenty of stalls selling everyday household objects. There's a great food market inside the large 18th century building in the square with a fantastic and very cheap restaurant called 'da Rocco' (basic and no-frills). A good choice for an authentic market experience.

Mercato delle Pulci ('flea market')
where   piazza dei Ciompi
when: last Sunday of the month

The Ciompi market is mainly an antique furniture market with some stands that also sell antique jewelry, paintings, old magazines and books and general artifacts and memorabilia from the past. A smaller version of the market is open Tue – Sat all year in the middle of the square and follows normal shop hours. Collectors and aficionados of antique furniture and old bric-a-brac will appreciate this market – others might not find it of much interest.

Fierucola Market
where   piazza Santo Spirito (walk there or mini-bus line 'D' direction 'Ferrucci', to 'Serragli' stop)
when: the third Sunday of each month 9 - 7 (not on in August)

A market selling organic foods and goods produced using biological agriculture (fruits and vegetables, bread, pizza, cakes, oil, jam, wine, cheeses, cold cuts). The 'fierucola' market is an homage to a simpler rural life and has many stalls selling hand made goods such as wool, cotton or linen knits, wood toys, jewelry, candles, soaps and lovely ceramics. Also vegan food stands.

www.lafierucola.org

Fortezza da Basso Market
where   the garden next to the Fortezza da Basso in Viale Strozzi (15 min. walk from station)
when: the third weekend of the month, 9 – 7 (not on in August)

A true flea market in the traditional sense of the term: vintage books and magazines, LP records and 45s, ceramics and porcelain, historical photos, old film posters, collectors items such as watches, cameras, phonographs, radios, telephones and jukeboxes, linens and embroidered goods, second-hand clothes and accessories, jewelry, antique furniture, Tiffany lamps and more.

Flea market and antiques
where piazza Santo Spirito (walk there or mini-bus line 'D' direction 'Ferrucci', to 'Serragli' stop)
when: the second Sunday of each month (not on in August)

Similar to the 'Fortezza da Basso' market (many of the stall owners are the same) only on a smaller scale. However, in piazza Santo Spirito the market has a much quainter and 'old world' ambience.

Flower market
where via Pellicceria (piazza della Repubblica) - under the arched portico
when: every Thursday 9 – 4

A lovely market which extends the length of the beautiful portico just near piazza Repubblica. There's a large selection of flowers and plants as well as seeds and other gardening items.

Markets in Piazza Santissima Annunziata:
Once a year the following single-theme markets are held in piazza Santissima Annunziata from 9 am – 7 pm.

- **Bread Market** – first weekend of September
- **Ceramics Market** – first weekend of October
- **Wool Market** – first weekend of November
- **Nativity Season Market** – first and second weekend of December

Fringe Shopping

If you want to have an even more authentic Florence shopping experience, you might consider **fringe shopping.**

These 'Fringe Shopping' pages tell you about popular shopping spots where locals go as an alternative to shopping downtown. Shopping in non-central neighborhoods means fewer crowds and a more authentic Florentine experience.

However, please bear in mind that not all shop assistants in the outer-areas will speak English so you might want to carry a phrase book. This could turn into a great occasion to practice your Italian, making your fringe visit even more of an authentic Florentine outing.

Please note when planning to fringe shop:

Unlike the center of Florence, the outer areas tend to observe traditional opening hours:

September – June
Mon morning closed. Shops open Mon 3.30 pm
Tue – Sat 9.30 – 1 and 3.30 - 7
Sundays closed

July – August
Mon - Fri 9.30 – 1 and 3.30 - 7
Sat morning only 9.30 – 1 afternoon closed
Sundays closed

Fringe area # 1 - Piazza Dalmazia

Piazza Dalmazia is a busy hub, and very popular shopping spot with Florentines. It has a real neighborhood feel with plenty of people hanging out in the square.   There's also an open air market every morning from 9 to 1 which sells clothes, shoes, house ware and plenty of different foods.

How to get there by bus:

Bus no. 14 (direction 'Tolentino' or 'Careggi') stops right in piazza Dalmazia square. You can get no. 14 in largo Alinari, at the pharmacy side of the station. From the station you go out (there'll be escalators on the far right) and cross the two streets at the traffic light. The bus stop is just near the traffic light in front of a pastry shop and 'Fabiani' jewelers.

There are many worthwhile shops and a large variety, so it's a good idea just to stroll around and see what catches your eye. However, here's a list of some of the most popular stores in the square and along the adjoining streets:

In Piazza Dalmazia square:

Grazia, no. 31r, ladies fashion, knitwear, classic and elegant styles
Calzature Marò, no. 29r, good quality reasonably prices shoes and bags (carries the marvelous Kipling brand)
Iana, no. 46r, kids clothes ages 0 -14

Delirio, no. 60, one of my favorite shops for fashionable women's clothes, shop assistant is always a big help so tell her what you're looking for. Trendy young styles.
Trombetta, no. 50r, refined elegant looks for mature ladies
Intimissimi, no. 39r undergarments and sleepwear

Casini Jewelers (since 1900), no. 43r, beautiful jewelry shop
Carpise, no. 63r, bags at low prices, good value
Oviesse (right in square) inexpensive department store (see chapter on 'Department Stores')

Just off the square in via Vittorio Emanuele:

Basimarò, no. 105a, high-quality ladies wear, elegant styles, worth a visit, higher-end prices

Just off the square in via Corridoni:

Fonderia, no 83, used to be a foundry, trendy clothes in New York loft-like atmosphere
Benetton, via Corridoni 34r casual clothes
Calzedonia, via Corridoni 27r hosiery
Mela Blu, 42r, herbal shop and environmentally friendly goods

Just off the square (across the small foot bridge) in via Reginaldo Giuliani:

Harold, no 8, elegant men's wear, refined classic line with a still casual feel, high end
Spada Erboristeria, no. 9r, herbal shop, nice hand made items in back area
Malizia, no 15r, ladies undergarments, pajamas, robes, knitwear

A little away from square, in viale Morgagni (wide tree-lined street):

Firenze Moda, no. 8c, men's and women's clothes, no brand names but good quality traditional pieces. Very big store with large selection and good prices, for the sensible practical shopper.

Where to eat in Piazza Dalmazia area:

Pit Stop, via Corridoni no. 30r, extremely popular pizzeria and restaurant, huge selection

Café Dalmazia, piazza Dalmazia no. 19r, coffee shop, home-made pastries, ice cream

Cafè de Paris, piazza Dalmazia no 7r, opens at 6 pm. Aperitif bar, buy a drink and eat from hot and cold buffet for free, from 6 pm til 8ish

Café D'Orzo, via Reginaldo Giuliani no 17 (just over foot bridge), an organic bar, cafè d'orzo means 'barley coffee' and here they serve healthy snacks, organic cakes, fruit shakes, fresh-squeezed fruit juices, herbal teas, soy milk cappuccino's, soy milk ice cream, sugar-free pastries

Gelateria Dalmazia, piazza Dalmazia, 37C (red), home-made ice cream

DOC, via Reginaldo Giuliani no 11r (just over foot bridge), wine bar, serves hot and cold lunches and Tuscan specialties.

Fringe area # 2 – Via Doni

Via Doni and the surrounding area is officially zoned as 'centro storico' although it is a bit off the beaten path for tourists. This is a smaller shopping area than Piazza Dalmazia which is growing in popularity – new shops and eateries are opening all the time.

How to get there by bus:

There are several buses that stop in this area. Either no. 17, direction 'Boito' or 'Cascine', which you can get at station near escalators-pharmacy side. Alternatively, buses no. 29, 30, or 35 which all stop in via Alamanni, on the tram side of the station. Bus stop is a block away from steps leading up to station entrance, walk in direction of the tram rails and via Alamanni is the street on the right when the road forks. Take any of these buses to the 'via Toselli' stop (there's a fenced-in parking lot right in front of the bus stop). From the bus stop walk back along via Toselli to the traffic light, on the left is via Doni (there's a 'Stefan' store on corner). Nicest shops start in the middle of via Doni.

<u>Popular shops and locales:</u>

Puzzle, via Doni 27r, street look clothes for guys and girls
Ballini & Carloni, via Monteverdi 28 (next door to 'Puzzle' on side street), jewelry and brand name designer silver and steel jewelry, very nice stuff
Easy Market, three stores in via Maragliano (no. 76 kids wear, 27r ladies, 73 men) just off via Doni.
A sort of mini-department store with large variety and reasonable prices. Classic looks for every day, good value
Mirella Mori, via Doni, 43c, ladies wear on the elegant side, frilly, lacy, flowery looks

Camilla, via Doni 83r, under garments, bathing suits, top quality
Baume & Mercer, via Doni 85r, watches, watch repair, jewelry and designer silver and steel jewelry
Vitalogy, via Doni 87r, Italian leather shoes, some Spanish labels too
Il Vento e la Seta, via Doni 34r, Italian clothes for women. More youthful styles than classic or traditional. Lots of fun clothes, lively patterns, form fitting, fur lined, ruffled sleeves, satin cuffs, this sort of thing.

Also in via Doni: shop for children's clothes and historical store for plus-sized clothes (**Ferrise Renzo**, via Doni 28r, since 1966).

Places to eat in via Doni area:

Sottozero, via Doni 47, very good ice cream and frozen yogurt
Pugi, via Doni 12r, a famous Florentine bakery, serves hot pizza by the piece (closed between 1 and 4 pm), great cakes too
Coffee Shop, via Doni 10r
Boutique del Cioccolato, via Maragliano 12c (red), a small gourmet chocolate shop and coffee house. Lots of yummy sweets and cakes and chocolate delicacies made in all sorts of shapes and designs.
La Taverna di Pietro, via Ponte alle Mosse 134r (off via 'Lulli'), extremely no-frills fish restaurant offering only a few basic dishes, but very tasty and inexpensive, opens at 7:30 pm – **only takes cash.**

Fringe area # 3 – Via Gioberti area:

Via Gioberti is a quite long street which goes from Piazza Beccaria to Piazza Alberti. It is one of the places that locals consider almost as good as shopping in the main downtown area because there is so much variety. The one downside is that it is quite cramped to walk around, the sidewalks are very narrow and there are tons of cars, bikes, scooters, etc. parked and whizzing around. The good side is that all the shops are concentrated on this one street.

The area offers both middle-range stores as well as high-end fashion. The best thing to do is walk from one end of the via to the other and just check out the stores whose shop windows interest you most. Doing both sides of the street this should take about 3 hours of leisurely shopping. There are many shops for shoes and clothes (girls, women, guys, men, and lots of children's wear too) and plenty of shops with designer names.

How to get there:

This is the fringe area that is closest to the center, so you could just walk there (from Borgo La Croce, cross Piazza Beccaria and go into via Gioberti). Otherwise, any bus that goes to or near Piazza Beccaria is fine (mini-buses C2 or C3 direction 'Beccaria' are probably the best since they are easily caught from downtown).

Some places worth mentioning in via Gioberti:

Serafini, via Gioberti 168r (just on left coming from Beccaria) coffee bar and pastry shop, great pastries as well as sandwiches and hot meals at lunchtime

Nath Nath, via Gioberti 103r a wonderful store for all made-in-Italy clothes for young and mature women. Comfortable free-flowing clothes. Store has extremely flattering clothes in plus-sizes too.

Chocolate shop Andrea Bianchini, the best chocolate specialist in Florence, pastries, cakes, bon bons, etc. (in the 'nove botteghe' shopping courtyard, go in through the archway near via Gioberti no. 61).

Outback Collection, via Gioberti, 32D/6 (inner courtyard area on the left) Spacious elegant store for girls and women, has both high-end classic styles as well as every day wear at lower prices

Bestock, via Gioberti 5f (almost at the piazza Alberti end), made-in-Italy clothes for girls and women. Both casual and slightly elegant styles mostly all in the stores self-produced 'Vida' label. Original designs and colors at great prices (the best probably in the whole street). Nice guy owns the shop who lets you get on with it undisturbed. Worth walking to the end of the street for.

Ang, via Gioberti 2dR (near Piazza Alberti end) baby and children's clothes (0 – 10 years) all made by hand by the Italian owner, Agnese. Very playful, colourful, imaginative outfits for kids. All natural fibres and very soft biological cotton for sensitive skin. Dresses start at €20.

& More...

The shops below are given short entries for the sole reason that I'm trying to keep this guide down to a manageable size. For their respective niches, these shops are first-rate.

Antique jewelry
MGB 6 in Condotta, via della Condotta, 6r   Jewelry dating from 1800 to 1960

Eye-glasses
Antica Occhialeria via San Gallo, 126r
Historic shop, vintage (sun)glasses
www.anticaocchialeria.com

Ferrari and Grand Prix memorabilia
Ferrari Store, via degli Strozzi, 4r tel. 055 23 99 125 (near piazza della Repubblica)
www.ferraristore.com
Everything, via Ricasoli, 121r cell. 334 351 52 61 (corner of piazza San Marco)

Gourmet foods
Pegna, v. dello Studio 8, best place for Italian and foreign specialty foods, in a palazzo from 1400s

Handcrafted Silver Jewelry
M.G., via Borgo Ognissanti 72r, tel. 055 26 82 64
www.mari-y-foglia.com **beautiful wedding rings**
Il Galeone, via Borgo Ognissanti 129r, tel. 055 05 02 727
www.giudicigioielli.com

Houseware
Bartolini, via dei Servi 72r, a fantastic store for the home, everything to do with cooking

Military items
Il Tricolore, via della Scala 25r, *www.iltricolore.it*   clothes and gear used by Italian armed forces

Model cars, boats, planes
Hobbitalia, via degli Artisti 11d/e, tel. 055 55 35 499 (near p. Donatello)

Silverware Frediano) historic shop for artisan silverware *www.brandimarte.com*

Soccer Jerseys
Soccertown, via Ricasoli 25r official merchandise of teams, not knock-offs seen all over town
Alè Viola, via del Corso 58r, tel. 055 29 53 06 *www.aleviola.net* Florence team store

Sportswear
Universosport, p. del Duomo 6r, tel. 055 28 44 12 also casual clothes and everyday wear

Toys
Bartolucci, via Condotta 6r, toys hand-made out of wood *www.bartolucci.com*
Dreoni (since 1922), via Cavour 31r, tel. 055 21 66 11 *www.dreonigiocattoli.eu*

Let's Fix It!

Laptop suddenly gone mad? Or worse, not working at all? Nothing's worse than needing technical assistance in a foreign country where you don't know who to turn to.

And more importantly, how can you know who to trust? We all know that foreigners can easily become prey to unscrupulous 'service providers', especially when dealing in expensive equipment like computers and cameras.

Here are the names of **trustworthy, honest** and **professional technical experts** for any camera or PC woes you may encounter:

Camera:
QSS Florence Center
Via Cavour 37r
055 28 82 11
fotoqss@libero.it

Computer:
Lomark Technology
Via G. Lulli 20r (parallel to via Doni)
Cell: 338 81 88 106 (Lorenzo)
Cell: 348 65 19 626 (Salvatore)
info@lomark.it

This small computer lab is 10 minutes from the downtown area by bus (no. 22 direction "Novoli" or 57 direction "Sesto Fiorentino", Maragliano stop) or car, but the service and extremely fair prices are worth the short trip.

A Presto!

I hope that you have enjoyed discovering Florence and its shopping scene through this guide.

If you have any comments or suggestions to make you would do me a huge favor by communicating them to me! Please either leave a comment on Amazon.com where you bought this book or contact me at www.florencewebguide.com using the 'Contact Me' page.

Grazie mille e ciao a presto!
Carol